THE MIRACLE OF LOVE

A GUIDE FOR CATHOLIC PASTORAL CARE

MARGARET GHOSN

COVENTRY PRESS

Published in Australia by
Coventry Press
33 Scoresby Road
Bayswater Vic. 3153
Australia

ISBN 9780648145738

Copyright © Margaret Ghosn 2018

All rights reserved. Other than for the purposes and subject to the conditions prescribed under the *Copyright Act*, no part of this publication may be reproduced, stored in a retrieval system, or transmitted in any form or by any means, electronic, mechanical, photocopying, recording or otherwise, without the prior permission of the publisher.

Scripture quotations are from the *New Revised Standard Version Bible*, copyright 1989, Division of Christian Education of the National Council of the Churches of Christ in the United States of America. Used by permission. All rights reserved.

First published 2018

Cataloguing-in-Publication entry is available from the National Library of Australia
http:/catalogue.nla.gov.au/.

Text design by Filmshot Graphics (FSG)
Cover design by Ian James – www.jgd.com.au

Printed in Australia

Contents

Introduction 5

Chapter 1: Scriptural basis for care 9

Chapter 2: The Church and the call to care 22

Chapter 3: Models of pastoral care today 37

Chapter 4: Do we really care anyway? 49

Chapter 5: Qualities of a pastoral carer 58

Chapter 6: Ethical dimension and self-care 75

Chapter 7: Meaning of suffering 87

Chapter 8: Times of crises 97

Chapter 9: Care of the young 111

Chapter 10: Care of the elderly 120

Chapter 11: Care of the sick 132

Chapter 12: Care of the dying 144

Chapter 13: Care of the grieving 161

Conclusion 177

Bibliography 180

Introduction

Recent movies by Kenneth Lonergan include *Margaret* and *Manchester by the Sea*. In both films, the main characters are in search of forgiveness but find it elusive because they can't forgive themselves. They are in a world that is too cold, too hard. The small inklings of care and hope that come their way are pushed aside until the end, when they can finally accept their own brokenness and that of those around them. Both are exceptional movies which provide stark examples of a world that can't forgive because it has no time in its busy lifestyle that chokes any attempt to receive care and forgiveness. It often feels like a dog eat dog world. Yet even this phrase seems outmoded by another recent animation at the box office, *Baby Boss*, where the idea of dogs earning the affections of adults in preference to babies gives us a reality check. Why have we lost the ability to care? Why don't we admit our failures or seek forgiveness? What are we chasing after and what is this world leading us to become?

When Jesus was asked what was the first and greatest commandment he recited the *Shema*, 'Hear O Israel: The Lord our God, the Lord is one; you shall love the Lord your God with all your heart, and with all your soul, and with all your mind, and with all your strength' (Mark 12:29). This commandment was familiar to Jewish ears (Deuteronomy 6:4-5). Before all else, one must put God first, to learn from God, to become like God and not just emotionally attached to God. By including 'with all your mind', Jesus implies that we must behave, choose, think over our words, motives and behaviour. We are accountable for everything we say and do.

The second commandment that follows is, 'You shall love your neighbour as yourself' (Mark 12:31) which again was common to Jewish ears (Leviticus 19:18). Taking this commandment on its own poses a problem. Is it saying the way we love ourselves must be reflected in the way we love our neighbour? Yet if we have little love for ourselves, then we will show the same disregard for others. Taking it further, if we are to measure everything according to our values and attitudes, that is if all things were subjectively based, then no one would reach their best potential. Jesus knew this and wisely said the first commandment is to focus and learn from God. That is our measuring stick. What then follows is the ability to love ourselves as God would have us be, and so love of neighbour becomes true acts of justice and mercy.

To ensure we were not to rely on our love as the measuring stick for love of others, Jesus also gave us a new commandment, 'Just as I have loved you, you also should love one another' (John 13:34). For us to love one another, we needed a concrete example and so Jesus set himself as the model – a challenge, but a necessary one.

Pastoral care doesn't come from one's own capacity to love because we are limited and prone to sin. True pastoral care originates from our relationship with Christ, through whom we have experienced love and hope, compassion and mercy. This is the source of our pastoral care.

The risk of writing about pastoral care is that it may sound like some warm, fuzzy feeling based solely on emotion and lots of hugs, lacking any real direction or depth. Of course, this is not the case, but for a society that measures the importance of something based on the criteria of success, wealth and popularity, then pastoral care may not appeal, as it is long term and very much reliant on the grace of God in people's lives. Furthermore, in Western society where reason and individualism, materialism and consumerism trump self-effacement and virtues, pastoral care lacks appeal, with its subtle and non-obtrusive methods. Yet it is a hidden power that reaps valuable and long-term success, for it awakens the often-untapped power of the spirit.

This book is for all, as a guide to understanding how care matters and is needed, not just by the one receiving care, but by givers too. It is about caregiving involving physical effort, practical assistance, spiritual wisdom, relationship development, faith nurturing, justice seeking and retelling of stories. It's about growing together and making the world we live in a more welcoming, forgiving and caring place, so that people will experience forgiveness and know love and be healed.

When I published my first book on pastoral care - *Instrument of your peace* (Preston: Challenge Books, 2012) - my intention was to offer my insights into various aspects of pastoral care from a Catholic perspective. This new book is more comprehensive, more researched, more practical with richer access to sources in the Bible and the Catholic tradition. My hope is that it will provide a much fuller introduction to pastoral care and be an encouragement to all who live this ministry in our Church.

Chapter 1: Scriptural basis for care

The Lord bless you and watch over you; the Lord make his face to shine upon you, and be gracious to you; the Lord look kindly upon you, and give you peace. - **Numbers 6:24-26**

Jesus the stranger was also a catalyst: he accelerated the pace of change, caused unimaginable reactions, offered unexpected alternatives, enabled healing to happen, precipitated novelty. People came to expect something exciting when he was around, and he in turn was excited by their faith-filled responses. Yet, no one could predict his actions any more than he could control their response to grace. Nevertheless, in this community, the reign of God was promoted. - **Anthony J Gittins**[1]

The Hebrew Scriptures

In the Book of Genesis, there is the understanding that God creates all with loving kindness, and God is fond of life: 'God saw everything that he had made, and indeed, it was very good' (Genesis 1:31). All life is blessed and all life is gift that finds its fulfilment in God. From the first two chapters of Genesis, we learn that the person is created in the image of God, a moral subject capable of selfdirection and selfdetermination through the exercise of freedom.

However, as the story unravels, humans find themselves in strife. Yet, despite the suffering caused by wrong decisions and toil that must be endured, God never forsakes man and woman, making, 'garments of skins for the man and his wife', (Genesis 3:21), clothing them and inviting them to reclaim their original goodness and beauty, as made in the image of God.

Genesis chapters 7-8 tell the story of Noah, who built the ark that saved a remnant from the chaos and devastation of the flood. In reference to the flood waters that carry Noah's family off, Margaret Silf sees it as a picture of transition, carried off by circumstances beyond

---

[1] Anthony J. Gittins, *Reading the Clouds. Mission Spirituality for New Times*, (Strathfield: St Pauls, 1999), 88

one's control into a world that seems full of threat and turbulence, and waving goodbye to everything left behind. The ark comes to rest on the top of Mount Ararat at a higher place than it could have reached had it not been carried there on the waters of apparent destruction. The rainbow is a silent, ever-recurring restatement of the promise that whatever chaos and breakdown occur in life, God will be present.[2]

As we continue through the Book of Genesis, we read how Abraham begs pardon for the sinners of Sodom (Genesis 18:16-33) despite their blatant desire for misconduct. It is in dire circumstances that care finds the courage to speak up and God was willing to listen to Abraham's plea. Again, we see the generous gift of care when Joseph forgives his brothers despite having been sold into slavery out of jealousy (Genesis 45:4-5), for care forgets all wrongs and hurts, in order to allow truth and peace to prevail.

In the Book of Exodus, we read of Moses and his muttering excuses to be the one to deliver the Hebrew people from slavery into God's care. He conveys the dread that is in many of us, 'But Moses said to God, "Who am I that I should go to Pharaoh, and bring the Israelites out of Egypt?"' (Exodus 3:11) and again in Exodus 3:13, 'What shall I say to them?' A third time Moses excuses himself, 'But suppose they do not believe me or listen to me' (4:1) Again we read of Moses' fear, 'O my Lord, I have never been eloquent, neither in the past nor even now that you have spoken to your servant; but I am slow of speech and slow of tongue' (4:10). A final time Moses pleads, 'O my Lord, please send someone else' (Exodus 4:13). Like Moses, we are not always confident of what we are capable of. Despite one's hesitancy, with time and the experience of God's compassion, one can become bearers of God's love, as we see with Moses' impassioned plea to save the people in Exodus 32:11-14 and again in Exodus 32:30-32:

> On the next day Moses said to the people, 'You have sinned a great sin. But now I will go up to the Lord; perhaps I can make atonement for your sin.' So Moses returned to the Lord and said, 'Alas, this people has sinned a great sin; they have made for themselves gods of gold. But now, if you will only

---

[2]Margaret Silf, *The other side of chaos. Breaking through when life is breaking down*, (Chicago: Loyola Press, 2011), 64-65, 68

forgive their sin—but if not, blot me out of the book that you have written.'

Where Moses was the voice for the people seeking God's care, Elijah the Prophet was the voice of God to a people who had strayed. Elijah insisted that the people, along with their king and queen, come to the realisation that life was to be lived in fidelity to the God who loves. It is this same prophet who continued time and time again to ensure that God's saving love reached the hearts and minds of people, as seen in raising a widow's only son (1 Kings 17:17-24).

Then there is Jonah's reluctance to bear God's words to others, choosing 'to flee to Tarshish from the presence of the Lord' (Jonah 1:3). However, God's desire for mercy cannot be ignored and Jonah returns to preach to the people of Nineveh. Upon their unexpected repentance, Jonah exclaimed 4:2-3:

'O Lord! Is not this what I said while I was still in my own country? That is why I fled to Tarshish at the beginning; for I knew that you are a gracious God and merciful, slow to anger, and abounding in steadfast love, and ready to relent from punishing. And now, O Lord, please take my life from me, for it is better for me to die than to live.'

Do we, like Jonah, harbour a darker side of ourselves that keeps us from freely offering compassion to others? Or do we rejoice over the mercy shown to others?

Moving through the Hebrew Scriptures (First Testament), we come across the prophets who articulate the compassion and mercy of a God who desires, above all, a loving and faithful relationship with people. Perhaps the most important passage is from Micah 6:8 which reads:

He has told you, O mortal, what is good; and what does the Lord require of you but to do justice, and to love kindness, and to walk humbly with your God?

This verse includes the call to work for justice and equality for all, to show compassion and kindness and love to those in need, and finally to know that all we do emerges from our relationship with God. There are also a number of other passages in the Prophetic writings that reflect God's care.

Isaiah 41:10 Do not fear, for I am with you, do not be afraid, for I am your God; I will strengthen you, I will help you, I will uphold you with my victorious right hand.

Isaiah 43:1, 4 But now thus says the Lord, he who created you, O Jacob, he who formed you, O Israel: Do not fear, for I have redeemed you; I have called you by name, you are mine... Because you are precious in my sight, and honoured, and I love you.

Isaiah 46:4 Even to your old age I am he, even when you turn grey I will carry you. I have made, and I will bear; I will carry and will save.

Isaiah 49:13 Sing for joy, O heavens, and exult, O earth; break forth, O mountains, into singing! For the Lord has comforted his people, and will have compassion on his suffering ones.

Isaiah 49:15-16 Can a woman forget her nursing-child, or show no compassion for the child of her womb? Even these may forget, yet I will not forget you. See, I have inscribed you on the palms of my hands.

Jeremiah 29:11 For surely I know the plans I have for you, says the Lord, plans for your welfare and not for harm, to give you a future with hope.

Hosea 11:1-4 When Israel was a child, I loved him, and out of Egypt I called my son. The more I called them, the more they went from me; they kept sacrificing to the Baals, and offering incense to idols. Yet it was I who taught Ephraim to walk, I took them up in my arms; but they did not know that I healed them. I led them with cords of human kindness, with bands of love. I was to them like those who lift infants to their cheeks. I bent down to them and fed them.

The Writings of the Hebrew Scriptures (Wisdom Books) have much to say in regards to one's relationship with God and the need to be at right with God and others. Again listed below are a number of passages from the Writings, one can reflect on.

Sirach 7:34 Fail not to be with them that weep, and mourn with them that mourn. Be not slow to visit the sick: for that shall make you to be beloved.

Psalm 8:3-4 When I look at your heavens, the work of your fingers, the moon and the stars that you have established; what are human beings that you are mindful of them, mortals that you care for them?

Psalm 23:1-2, 6 The Lord is my shepherd, I shall not want. He makes me lie down in green pastures; he leads me beside still waters; he restores my soul . . . Surely goodness and mercy shall follow me all the days of my life, and I shall dwell in the house of the Lord my whole life long.

Psalm 30:2 I cried to you for help, O Lord my God, and you healed me.

Psalm 46:1 God is our refuge and strength, a very present help in trouble.

Psalm 147:3 He heals the broken-hearted, and binds up their wounds.

From the journey of the Israelites into faith, we leave the Hebrew Scriptures and enter into the Christian Scriptures (Second Testament), and the story of Jesus, our pastoral care model.

Jesus in the Gospels

In Jesus, we witness the best of humanity. He exhibited generosity of heart, sensitivity towards the needy, compassion to those in despair, and infinite love towards neighbour. He loved and healed, listened and responded, comforted and forgave. People approached him because there was nothing to fear, 'He will not break a bruised reed nor quench a smouldering wick' (Matthew 12:20; Isaiah 42:3).

Jesus attended to people who were hurting physically, socially, mentally and spiritually through miraculous healings, forgiveness of sins, and casting out demons. Jesus' miracles freed people from suffering, restored personal integrity, and reassured them that God was at work in their lives. Anthony Gittins writes of Jesus:

> He will speak of God's compassion for every single person, and God's utter lack of vindictiveness or partiality. He will preach good news of community and inclusion and hope to a people steeped in a world of hierarchy and exclusion and fatalistic despair. This will bring upon him the opprobrium and self-righteousness of the privileged classes. It will also have such liberating potential for despised and condemned people as to give them a new lease on life, turning at least some of them into a community of radical itinerants or healed healers.[3]

---

[3] Anthony J. Gittins *Reading the Clouds. Mission Spirituality for New Times*, (Strathfield: St Pauls, 1999), 111

Jesus' care is seen throughout the Gospels. Such examples follow, with verses in italics highlighting his care:

Mark 1:40-41 A leper came to him begging him, and kneeling he said to him, 'If you choose, you can make me clean.' *Moved with pity, Jesus stretched out his hand and touched him, and said to him, 'I do choose. Be made clean!'*

Mark 1:29-31 As soon as they left the synagogue, they entered the house of Simon and Andrew, with James and John. Now Simon's mother-in-law was in bed with a fever, and they told him about her at once. *He came and took her by the hand and lifted her up.* Then the fever left her, and she began to serve them.

Luke 7:11-15 Soon afterwards he went to a town called Nain, and his disciples and a large crowd went with him. As he approached the gate of the town, a man who had died was being carried out. He was his mother's only son, and she was a widow; and with her was a large crowd from the town. *When the Lord saw her, he had compassion for her and said to her, 'Do not weep.'* Then he came forward and touched the bier, and the bearers stood still. And he said, 'Young man, I say to you, rise!' The dead man sat up and began to speak, and Jesus gave him to his mother.

Luke 8:35 Then people came out to see what had happened, and *when they came to Jesus, they found the man from whom the demons had gone sitting at the feet of Jesus,* clothed and in his right mind. And they were afraid.

Mark 8:1-3 In those days when there was again a great crowd without anything to eat, he called his disciples and said to them, *'I have compassion for the crowd,* because they have been with me now for three days and have nothing to eat. If I send them away hungry to their homes, they will faint on the way - and some of them have come from a great distance.'

Mark 7:32-34 They brought to him a deaf man who had an impediment in his speech; and they begged him to lay his hand on him. *He took him aside in private, away from the crowd,* and put his fingers into his ears, and he spat and touched his tongue. Then looking up to heaven, he sighed and said to him, 'Ephphatha', that is, 'Be opened.'

Mark 8:22-25 They came to Bethsaida. Some people brought a blind man to him and begged him to touch him. *He took the blind man by the hand and led him out of the village;* and when he had put saliva on his eyes and laid his hands on him, he asked him, 'Can you see anything?' And the man looked up and said, 'I can see people, but they look like trees, walking.' Then Jesus laid his hands on his eyes again; and he looked intently and his sight was restored, and he saw everything clearly.

Mark 10:20-21 He said to him, 'Teacher, I have kept all these since my youth.' *Jesus, looking at him, loved him* and said, 'You lack one thing; go, sell what you own, and give the money to the poor, and you will have treasure in heaven; then come, follow me.'

John 8:7-11 Jesus bent down and wrote with his finger on the ground. When they kept on questioning him, he straightened up and said to them, 'Let anyone among you who is without sin be the first to throw a stone at her.' And once again he bent down and wrote on the ground. When they heard it, they went away, one by one, beginning with the elders; and Jesus was left alone with the woman standing before him. Jesus straightened up and said to her, 'Woman, where are they? Has no one condemned you?' She said, 'No one, sir.' And *Jesus said, 'Neither do I condemn you.* Go your way, and from now on do not sin again.'

John 5:5-8 One man was there who had been ill for thirty-eight years. *When Jesus saw him lying there and knew that he had been there a long time, he said to him, 'Do you want to be made well?'* The sick man answered him, 'Sir, I have no one to put me into the pool when the water is stirred up; and while I am making my way, someone else steps down ahead of me.' Jesus said to him, 'Stand up, take your mat and walk.'

John 13:3-5 Jesus, knowing that the Father had given all things into his hands, and that he had come from God and was going to God, got up from the table, took off his outer robe, and tied a towel around himself. Then *he poured water into a basin and began to wash the disciples' feet* and to wipe them with the towel that was tied around him.

Matthew 23:37 'Jerusalem, Jerusalem, the city that kills the prophets and stones those who are sent to it! *How often have I desired to gather your children together as a hen gathers her brood under her wings, and you were not willing!*'

John 13:35 *Just as I have loved you, you also should love one another. By this everyone will know that you are my disciples, if you have love for one another.*

Jesus called the despised and the outcasts to join him, he defended the weak and vulnerable, accepted invitations to meals, enjoyed company, took time out to be with people, told stories, listened intently, demanded justice, wept at the death of a loved one, washed feet, and offered bread and wine to share, all acts that caringly awakened the heart of those he encountered. He was a man totally dedicated to creating a world inclusive of all – a world that cares.

Pope Francis writes about the importance of compassion and attending not only to the spiritual but also the physical needs of others. He uses the miracle of the multiplication of loaves and fish (Matthew 14:13-21) as his example:[4]

> We can understand three messages from this event. The first is *compassion* . . . He reacts with a feeling of compassion, because he knows they are not seeking him out of curiosity but out of need. But attention: compassion — which Jesus feels — is not simply feeling pity; it's more! It means to *suffer with*, in other words to empathise with the suffering of another, to the point of taking it upon oneself. Jesus is like this: he suffers together with us, he suffers with us, he suffers for us. And the sign of this compassion is the healing of countless people he performed. Jesus teaches us to place the needs of the poor before our own. Our needs, even if legitimate, are not as urgent as those of the poor, who lack the basic necessities of life. We often speak of the poor. But when we speak of the poor, do we sense that this man or that woman or those children lack the bare necessities of life? That they have no food, they have no

---

[4] Pope Francis, *Angelus*, St. Peter's Square, Sunday, 3 August 2014
https://w2.vatican.va/content/francesco/en/angelus/2014/documents/papa-francesco_angelus_20140803.html

clothing, they cannot afford medicine.... Also that the children do not have the means to attend school. Whereas our needs, although legitimate, are not as urgent as those of the poor who lack life's basic necessities.

The second message is *sharing*... The disciples think it would be better to send them away so they can go and buy food. Jesus instead says: 'you give them something to eat'. Two different reactions, which reflect two contrasting outlooks: the disciples reason with worldly logic, by which each person must think of himself; they reason as if to say: 'Sort it out for yourselves'. Jesus reasons with God's logic, which is that of sharing. How many times we turn away so as not to see our brothers in need! And this looking away is a polite way to say, with white gloves, 'Sort it out for yourselves'. And this is not Jesus' way: this is selfishness. Had he sent away the crowds, many people would have been left with nothing to eat. Instead those few loaves and fish, shared and blessed by God, were enough for everyone. And pay heed! It isn't magic, it's a 'sign': a sign that calls for faith in God, provident Father, who does not let us go without "our daily bread", if we know how to share it as brothers.

Compassion, sharing. And the third message: the miracle of the loaves foreshadows the *Eucharist*. It is seen in the gesture of Jesus who, before breaking and distributing the loaves, "blessed" them (Matthew 14:19). It is the same gesture that Jesus was to make at the Last Supper, when he established the perpetual memorial of his Redeeming Sacrifice.

So if we are to take Jesus as our role model for pastoral care then we are called to:
- Offer insight and wisdom
- Listen
- Empower
- Encourage
- Guide
- Heal

- Love
- Forgive
- Understand
- Be gentle
- Touch the heart
- Transform
- Seek justice
- Set minds at ease
- Be present for the other
- Advocate for change in the system
- Lead others to truth

We can summarise Jesus' attitude to one and all when he says, 'Come to me, all who labour and are heavy laden, and I will give you rest; for I am gentle and lowly in heart, and you will find rest for your souls' (Matthew 11:28-29). In Jesus, one is at peace, minds are settled, hearts are warmed, for there is nothing to fear.

Jesus taught in parables that people might understand. The call to be merciful is clearly witnessed in the parable 'The Judgment Day' (Matthew 25:34-40). We are called to go forth to feed the hungry, give drink to the thirsty, welcome the stranger, clothe the naked, visit the sick, visit the marginalised members of society, and come to those in prison (Matthew 25:35-36).

In the parable of the vineyard workers (Matthew 20:1-16), the owner is desperate to get his harvest in. As Barbara Reid explains, if the vineyard owner gives the workers who came last any less than the minimum to be able to feed their families at the end of the day, what good is that? Everybody deserves to eat at the end of the day and it doesn't depend on how long you have worked.[5] Like God, our care must extend to the very least and our care is to provide them with at least the basic necessities of life.

Jesus' coming into this world reveals a God who abandons status and dignity for the sake of humankind. Jesus loves to the point of laying down his life for his friends. The Resurrection appearances offer us a

---

[5]Barbara E Reid, 'In her shoes' in *U.S. Catholic*, January 2017:22

Jesus who returns to be with us, to nurture our trust. If the Resurrected Jesus can still be a God of love and tenderness, we can be assured that this God is unchanging.

Christian Scriptures

Other passages to reflect on in the Christian Scriptures (Second Testament) in regards to the Christian calling to care include exhortations from Paul and others:

Romans 12:9-15 Let love be genuine; hate what is evil, hold fast to what is good; love one another with mutual affection; outdo one another in showing honour. Do not lag in zeal, be ardent in spirit, serve the Lord. Rejoice in hope, be patient in suffering, persevere in prayer. Contribute to the needs of the saints; extend hospitality to strangers. Bless those who persecute you; bless and do not curse them. Rejoice with those who rejoice, weep with those who weep.

2 Corinthians 1:3-5 Blessed be the God and Father of our Lord Jesus Christ, the Father of mercies and the God of all consolation, who consoles us in all our affliction, so that we may be able to console those who are in any affliction with the consolation with which we ourselves are consoled by God. For just as the sufferings of Christ are abundant for us, so also our consolation is abundant through Christ.

2 Corinthians 11:29 Who is weak, and I am not weak? Who is made to stumble, and I am not indignant?

Galatians 6:2 Bear one another's burdens, and in this way you will fulfil the law of Christ.

Hebrews 13:3 Remember those who are in prison, as though you were in prison with them; those who are being tortured, as though you yourselves were being tortured.

1 Peter 4:8-11 Above all, maintain constant love for one another, for love covers a multitude of sins. Be hospitable to one another without complaining. Like good stewards of the manifold grace of God, serve one another with whatever gift each of you has received. Whoever speaks must do so as one speaking the very words of God; whoever serves must do so with the strength that God supplies, so that God may be glorified in all things through Jesus Christ.

1 John 4:7 Beloved, let us love one another, because love is from God; everyone who loves is born of God and knows God.

Our understanding of God is at the heart of our ministry and determines the way we offer care to others. In reflecting on the Scriptures, God is depicted as the One who came to care and calls us to do the very same.

Reflection

To be made in your image God,
Is to know you, love you and to be you.
You are God who chooses us.
The God who searches for the lost.
The God who sets us free.
The God who loves unconditionally.
The God who hears the cry of the poor.
The God who heals the blind, the sick and the lame.
The God who listens and answers prayers.
The God who laughs and weeps.
The God who enjoys company.
The God who blesses the young and old.
The God who generously gives.
The God who is always here for us.
The God who sees all, hears all and knows all.
The God who forgives time and time again.
The God who knows suffering, grief and death.
The God whose eternal light sustains our hope.
We too are called to be this same image.
God, make us people who care, who are moved with compassion,
who offer ourselves totally with love. Amen.

Chapter 2:
The Church and the call to care

If the world despises a notorious sinner, the church will love her. If the world cuts off aid to the poor and the suffering, the church will offer food and healing. If the world oppresses, the church will raise up the oppressed. If the world shames a social outcast, the church will proclaim God's reconciling love. If the world seeks profit and self-fulfilment, the church seeks sacrifice and service. If the world demands retribution, the church dispenses grace. If the world splinters into factions, the church joins together in unity. If the world destroys its enemies, the church loves them. - **Philip Yancey**[6]

The real question is, Who is the Church? You are the heart and centre of the very word Church. If we are to be church then I know that I need you, to stand next to me, a God with skin. I need to hear your voice being raised with mine in prayer. I need to know by the experience of your nearness that God has made you my sister, my brother, and that we are together God's family. I need to pray with you for the coming of the kingdom. God reaches out to me through you and out to you through me.

- **John Powell with Michael H Cheney**[7]

Pastoral care has been at the heart of the Church's mission for over two millennia in looking after the needs of the young and old, women and men. Originally, the term 'pastoral care' had its origins in 'to pastor,' meaning 'to look after and ensure the safety of one's cattle or livestock.' The shepherding imagery of ministry is seen throughout the Scriptures, including:

Psalm 23:1 The Lord is my shepherd, I shall not want.

Isaiah 40:11 He will feed his flock like a shepherd; he will gather the lambs in his arms, and carry them in his bosom, and gently lead the mother sheep.

---

[6]Philip Yancey, *What's so amazing about grace?* (Grand Rapids: Zondervan, 2000), 262.
[7]John Powell with Michael H Cheney, *A Life-Giving Vision: How to be a Christian in Today's world*, (Texas: Thomas More, 1995), 315.

Jeremiah 31:10 Hear the word of the Lord, O nations, and declare it in the coastlands far away; say, 'He who scattered Israel will gather him, and will keep him as a shepherd a flock.'

Matthew 18:12-14 What do you think? If a shepherd has a hundred sheep, and one of them has gone astray, does he not leave the ninety-nine on the mountains and go in search of the one that went astray? And if he finds it, truly I tell you, he rejoices over it more than over the ninety-nine that never went astray. So it is not the will of your Father in heaven that one of these little ones should be lost.

John 21:15-17 When they had finished breakfast, Jesus said to Simon Peter, 'Simon son of John, do you love me more than these?' He said to him, 'Yes, Lord; you know that I love you.' Jesus said to him, 'Feed my lambs.' A second time he said to him, 'Simon son of John, do you love me?' He said to him, 'Yes, Lord; you know that I love you.' Jesus said to him, 'Tend my sheep.' He said to him the third time, 'Simon son of John, do you love me?' Peter felt hurt because he said to him the third time, 'Do you love me?' And he said to him, 'Lord, you know everything; you know that I love you.' Jesus said to him, 'Feed my sheep.'

Acts 20:28 Keep watch over yourselves and over all the flock, of which the Holy Spirit has made you overseers, to shepherd the church of God that he obtained with the blood of his own Son.

1 Peter 5:2-4 To tend the flock of God that is in your charge, exercising the oversight, not under compulsion but willingly, as God would have you do it—not for sordid gain but eagerly. Do not lord it over those in your charge, but be examples to the flock. And when the chief shepherd appears, you will win the crown of glory that never fades away.

Revelation 7:17 For the Lamb at the centre of the throne will be their shepherd, and he will guide them to springs of the water of life, and God will wipe away every tear from their eyes.

Other longer references include Jeremiah 23:1-6, Ezekiel 34:1-24, Zechariah 11:4-17 and John 10:1-18. However, while rich in symbolism, the idea of a shepherd caring for the sheep can foster a sense of paternalism and judgmentalism, assuming the 'flock' are ignorant and dependent. Yet, the shepherding image is much more than watching over and protecting. It is in fact risky and challenging, exhausting and demanding. If we take the shepherd imagery, it involved being exposed to nature's wild elements, the heat and cold, threatened by predators and diseases. Armed with only a staff and know-how, it required vigilance day and night, over large flocks that were likely to lose their way and vulnerable to any prey. These sheep were under the care of the shepherd because they were of value to their owners.

Perhaps the shepherd image today is too distant from our present context, with our experience of living in the comfort of our homes, but the essence of shepherding, of pastoral care, remains with ideals of responsibility, of weathering storms, of patient watching over those in need of care. In spite of today's emphasis on individualism and independence, there is always a time where we could do with a bit of help, someone to care for us, to watch over our safety and protect us from harm. We all have a purpose in life we must fulfil and that purpose will at times knock us to our knees, and at other times, allow us to grin with pride. We can at times feel like amateurs needing guidance and at other times like a leader guiding others. We are at times a shepherd, giving care, and at other moments, the sheep, needing care.

When Jesus says, 'I am sending you out like sheep into the midst of wolves' (Matthew 10:16), he puts a new twist on the understanding of pastoral care. Jesus also insists we are to 'be wise as serpents and innocent as doves' (Matthew 10:16). Faith is not to be placid, ignorant or irrelevant. It must develop, grow to challenge society's norms and offer depth and wisdom that can confidently address any rhetoric of subtle lies that want to dissuade from truth. This understanding of pastoral care extends into the arena of advocacy and social justice.

However, let us for now return to the original understanding of shepherding and pastoral care and trace the development up to current times. In the Hebrew Scriptures, pastoral leaders were seen in the priests and prophets, who were the wise guides and caretakers of the moral life of the people. In the Christian Scriptures, not only did Jesus heal but he summoned his twelve disciples to cast out unclean spirits, 'and to cure every disease and every sickness' (Matthew 10:1). It is the call to serve in every possible way. When Jesus calls the twelve to ministry, he calls all, for among the twelve were all sorts of people

- fishermen, tax collectors, siblings - and one who would betray him. The pastoral ministry to which Jesus calls his disciples and each of us has no selection criteria, but is a 'summons.' As a follower of Christ, there are expectations we must live up to, no matter who we are. That expectation is to offer care to others.

Jesus also said, 'For you always have the poor with you' (Matthew 26:11). What is imperative is not to forget, ignore or overlook the needs of others. Pastoral care is about making lives better, to remove where possible obstacles to growth, advocating for change, offering compassion and tenderness, unburdening others, alleviating suffering, to forgive past hurts, bandage wounds, to speak on behalf of the voiceless, to oppose any sort of oppression, to comfort with words and touch.

In the early Church, the leaders Peter, the Apostles and Paul, were entrusted with the mission of looking after God's holy flock by announcing the good news to all, forming communities, instructing and healing. A few quotes from Scripture give an indication of the form pastoral care took.

Mark 6:13 They cast out many demons, and anointed with oil many who were sick and cured them.

Luke 9:1 Then Jesus called the twelve together and gave them power and authority over all demons and to cure diseases.

Luke 10:1, 8-9 After this the Lord appointed seventy others and sent them on ahead of him in pairs to every town and place where he himself intended to go. Whenever you enter a town and its people welcome you, eat what is set before you; cure the sick who are there, and say to them, 'The kingdom of God has come near to you.'

Luke 24:47 And that repentance and forgiveness of sins is to be proclaimed in his name to all nations, beginning from Jerusalem.

Acts 2:38 Peter said to them, 'Repent, and be baptised every one of you in the name of Jesus Christ so that your sins may be forgiven; and you will receive the gift of the Holy Spirit.'

Acts 3:6-8 But Peter said, 'I have no silver or gold, but what I have I give you; in the name of Jesus Christ of Nazareth, stand up and walk.' And he took him by the right hand and raised him up; and immediately his feet and ankles were made strong. Jumping up, he stood and began to walk, and he entered the temple with them, walking and leaping and praising God.

Acts 6:8 Stephen, full of grace and power, did great wonders and signs among the people.

Acts 19:11 God did extraordinary miracles through Paul.

Perhaps the best summary of the pastoral care that occurred in the early church is seen in the Acts of the Apostles:

> They devoted themselves to the apostles' teaching and fellowship, to the breaking of bread and the prayers.
>
> Awe came upon everyone, because many wonders and signs were being done by the apostles. All who believed were together and had all things in common; they would sell their possessions and goods and distribute the proceeds to all, as any had need. Day by day, as they spent much time together in the temple, they broke bread at home and ate their food with glad and generous hearts, praising God and having the goodwill of all the people. And day by day the Lord added to their number those who were being saved. - **Acts 2:42-47**

It is worth noting from this passage that pastoral care was not just an individual summons, but the combined effort of a community, the call of all church members.

The Council at Jerusalem in 49 CE dealt with Gentile converts. Here rose the Justification through Faith argument put forward by Paul, that Christian life came through proclamation in Jesus and through baptism. He argued that concentrating on external rituals and Jewish practices were not vital. It was care of the person's soul and deep understanding of Christ that should be central in the life of a believer.

As time went by in the early Christian Church (100-476), institutionalism and sacerdotalism emerged in the second generation churches, resulting in the development of the offices of bishops, elders and deacons. In the earliest traditions the terms 'overseer' *(episkopos)*, which is usually translated bishop and elder *(presbyteros)* were used for those in charge of the community. They were judges when disputes arose between individuals and an instrument of the saving grace of God. The term deacon was used for those who played a role in assisting them (Philippians 1:1). These offices represented a departure from the original ministry of Jesus.

The Christian Scriptures tell of ministers being responsible for administration and spiritual guidance (Acts 15:6, 1 Timothy 5:17, James 5:14, 1 Peter 5:1-4, Acts 20:17, Ephesians 4:12 and Titus 1:5-7), oversight and leadership (Acts 20:28, Philippians 1:1, 1 Timothy 3:2-5, Titus 1:7, Acts 20:17, 1 Peter 5:1-2 and Titus 1:5-7), proclamation of the gospel and teaching of the flock (Romans 10:14, 1 Timothy 2:7, 2 Timothy 1:11), to feed (1 Peter. 5:2), edify (2 Corinthians 13:10), pray (Colossians 1:9), watch for souls (Hebrews 13:17), convince (Titus 1:9), comfort (2 Corinthians 1:4-6), rebuke (Titus 1:13), warn (Acts 20:31), admonish (2 Thessalonians 3:15) and exhort (Titus 1:9, 2:15).

From here onwards, the understanding of pastoral care would shift and change time and time again. The Church had to deal with the issue of post-baptismal sin and the question of readmission of apostates, those who had defected from the Christian community under the Roman persecution. As a result, the Church gradually developed a whole discipline of public and private penance. These aspects centred on Mass, sacraments, and on the Church and the priest as the teacher. There was also the pervading sense of sin, guilt, confession and avoiding hell.

In the Church of the third century onwards, the bishops were understood as those charged with the mission to feed God's holy flock, look for the lost sheep and heal the broken with love and mercy. Pastoral care revolved around church leaders and their duties to establish communion, console in times of turmoil and to visit the sick and needy.

According to William Clebsch and Charles Jaekle, the primary objective of pastoral care in the early church up to the year 180 was that of *sustaining*; during the time of persecution that of *reconciling*; and during the time of Constantine that of *guiding*.[8]

The fourth century registers the creation of hospices for pilgrims, and the beginning of the monastic tradition in caring for the sick.

Pope Gregory the Great (540-604), in his *Book of Pastoral Rule,* addressed issues, including duties of ministers towards the poor, sad, foolish, sick and others.

---

[8]William A. Clebsch and Charles R. Jaekle, *Pastoral Care in Historical Perspective* (New York: John Aronson, 1983), 11-31.

The western medieval church (476-1500) focused on the authority and celibacy of its clergy. Many retreated to the ascetic life of the monastery to escape worldliness. However, John Wycliffe (1324-1384), the leading Oxford scholar of his day, wrote, 'restrict the charter of the preacher to the expounding of Scripture,' and stated that 'priests should exercise their primary function, namely, pastoral care. They should not lurk in cloisters.'

In the Middle Ages, the sacramental, liturgical, ritualistic expression of care saw the minister as the physician of the soul, seeking to understand the deepest longings and the secret sins and fears of the people, so that healing could occur.

The twelfth century onwards saw the birth of hospital Orders and growth of lay confraternities committed to the development of health care structures to care for the sick and abandoned, and to address problems of the plague, leprosy and war. These included:

- The Order of Knights of the Hospital of Saint John of Jerusalem, that continued into the contemporary Sovereign Military Order of Malta we have today.
- The Hospitallers arose in the early 12th century, to provide care for sick, poor or injured pilgrims coming to the Holy Land.
- The Camillians or Clerics Regular, founded in 1582 by Saint Camillus de Lellis (1550-1614), taught that the 'hospital was a house of God, a garden where the voices of the sick were music from heaven'. The members of the Order wore upon their black cassocks a large red cross, which was later adopted as the international symbol of Red Cross.

The seventeenth century was marked by the figure of St Vincent de Paul who founded the Daughters of Charity to live the values of the Gospel in the care of the sick.

In the eighteenth century onwards, the Church was seen by the State as an obstacle and efforts were undertaken to marginalise it. The nineteenth century saw the emergence of the Industrial revolution and scientific developments. Social Action became the key word.

In the Second Vatican Council (1962-1965) document *Gaudium et Spes*, the opening words were a call to meet God in every human encounter:

The joys and the hopes, the griefs and the anxieties of the men (and women) of this age, especially those who are poor or in any way afflicted, these are the joys and hopes, the griefs and anxieties of the followers of Christ. Indeed, nothing genuinely human fails to raise an echo in their hearts.

The current leader of the Catholic Church, Pope Francis, has made pastoral care an essential task of the Church today, stating:

> I see clearly that the thing the church needs most today is the ability to heal wounds and to warm the hearts of the faithful; it needs nearness, proximity. I see the church as a field hospital after battle. It is useless to ask a seriously injured person if he has high cholesterol and about the level of his blood sugars! You have to heal his wounds. Then we can talk about everything else. Heal the wounds, heal the wounds.[9]

Thomas Groome notes that characteristics of the Catholic Church which contribute to its ministry of pastoral care include:

- *Leitourgia:* To worship God publicly as an assembly of Christian people, celebrating God's covenant in Christ and the hope of salvation for all (a worshipping community).

- *Diakonia:* to care for human needs – spiritual, psychological, and physical – helping to build up God's reign of peace and justice in the world, with special favour for the poor and disadvantaged (a community of welfare).

- *Marturia:* to bear credible public witness to Christian faith through living as an effective symbol of God's reign to the point of suffering and death (a witnessing community).[10]

He also sees Catholicism's emphasis on commitment, community, conversation, compassion, celebration and lifelong conversion, patterned on the intimacy of Christ with his Father.

So, over the centuries, pastoral care took on various forms. The negative pastoral roles that emerged over time included individualism, clericalism, paternalism, devotionalism, formalism, authoritarianism and sacramentalism.

---

[9]Antonio Spadaro, 'A Big Heart Open to God. The exclusive interview with Pope Francis' in *Thinking Faith. The online Journal of British Jesuits.* www.thinkingfaith.org 19th September 2013, 7.
[10]Thomas Groome, *What makes us Catholic. Eight gifts for life,* (NY: Harper San Francisco, 2002), 120.

The positive pastoral roles included works of mercy, admonishing the sinner, instructing and comforting, bearing wrong patiently, forgiving injuries, praying for the living and the departed, spiritual guidance, facilitator, evangeliser, educator and celebrant.

The pastoral task of the Church today is to help reflect, find meaning, and respond in ways that express the sacred dimensions of everyday life for individuals and communities that face challenges, moral dilemmas and tragedies. The Church draws upon stories, symbols, rituals and traditions of the Christian faith in its pastoral care.

Sacramental dimension

Jesus was a living sacrament of God's compassion. Today, the sacraments are symbolic actions in which believers are drawn into the mystery and salvation of Christ. They are expressions by the assembled church, to make accessible the saving work of Christ to all and encounters with the infinite mercy of God, that can heal brokenness. The sacraments also provide a way of living distinguished by freedom, hope and love, as well as an ethical and social consciousness.

The Sacrament of Baptism

The rite of baptism is the sign of new life with Christ. It is not just becoming children of God but living as Christ did and 'sharing his suffering' by becoming united as one with the anguish, fears and suffering of others as Romans 8:16-17 notes:

> it is that very Spirit bearing witness with our spirit that we are children of God, and if children, then heirs, heirs of God and joint heirs with Christ—if, in fact, we suffer with him so that we may also be glorified with him.

The baptised are pardoned, cleansed, sanctified and given a new ethical orientation under the Holy Spirit. In Baptism, grace flows, meaning is given, belonging is sensed, vocation is experienced, community as the Body of Christ is discovered, but so is calling and responsibility.

Remembering that Jesus' ministry commenced at his baptism, the Christian also embarks on a life long journey with the gifts of the Holy Spirit to assist, 'love, joy, peace, patience, kindness, generosity, faithfulness, gentleness and self-control' (Galatians 5:22-23). These gifts enable a baptised Christian to live more fully as a child of God and as disciples of care to others, being a 'light for the world' (Matthew 5:14).

Sacrament of the Eucharist

> Then he took a loaf of bread, and when he had given thanks, he broke it and gave it to them, saying, 'This is my body, which is given for you. Do this in remembrance of me.' - **Luke 22:19**

In the assembled people and the gifts prepared, hopes, joys and problems are presented, through thanksgiving, memorial and petition. Celebrating the Eucharist liturgy as one who is sick or suffering, or one who comes to serve and heal, or one who comes with grief and sorrow, allows for an increased capacity for suffering, hope and compassion and deeper gratitude and awe for each person gathered around the table of God. As Anthony J. Gittins writes:

> The Eucharist of Jesus (the formal institution) took place at table in the Upper Room the night before he died. His actions there are themselves a recapitulation, a concentration or distillation of his entire life. His entire outpouring ministry and outpouring death are concrete expressions of feeding, nurturing, healing, restoring, and attending to others' needs - in short, Eucharist that is relatively informal, spontaneous, variegated, and deeply relevant to actual lives and circumstances. . . The mission of the Church is to 'do *this*' in memory of Jesus. What exactly is *this*? We do not simply 'remember' as in 'call to mind' or 'evoke,' and we are certainly not told to mimic the actions of Jesus at the table, much less to repeat the unique sacrifice of Calvary. Anamnesis entails active remembering. That is more like 're-member-ing': 'putting the members back together', 'reproducing', or 're-embodying' in our own lives and communities some vital past experience. It is as if Jesus is saying urgently, 'keep me alive in your own lives; do not forget me but re-member me; come together and do *this* - everything I did for you - in your lives, as my legacy and as your own commitment.' *This* is what we must do, lest in failing to re-member, we actually forget.[11]

---

[11] Anthony J. Gittins, *Called to be sent. Co-Missioned as Disciples Today*, (Missouri: Liguori, 2008), 64-65

The Eucharist is given to us so that Christ's presence may be real, living in our attitudes and values, in our thinking, speaking and lifestyle. In receiving the Eucharist at the altar, we are then sent forth to enter into relationships lovingly, to be at the bedside of an ailing person, to offer Christ's presence to those who hunger and thirst for peace. The Eucharist nourishes us in our role as pastoral carers who come to see the world's brokenness, who give thanks for what is and what will be, who share the cup of suffering with our neighbour, who remind others of the God who never forgets us.

Sacrament of Reconciliation

Each person is created in the image of God. Whatever impedes that unfolding and development can be described as evil. The understanding of the sacrament of reconciliation is that the offer of mercy and forgiveness is available and waiting to be poured out by a God, who is 'waiting to be gracious to you' (Isaiah 30:18).

Neil Ormerod writes that we are drawn to the sacrament of reconciliation because of the experience of divine mercy and compassion. In reconciliation, not only are the sins people commit forgiven, but also their sense of estrangement from God, and hostility to the world is healed with acknowledgment and compassion.[12]

As a pastoral carer, one is called to offer the experience of God's forgiveness and love in order to allow others to overcome their guilt and estrangement. This is achieved by being 'kind to one another, tender-hearted, forgiving one another, as God in Christ has forgiven you' (Ephesians 4:32). When one is open to receive the gift of forgiveness, one experiences a profound peace. As Elizabeth Lee writes:

> We begin our ritual. Over the next hour and a half Simon, a man of 45, shares his story – initially disclosing petty things he has done, then bit by bit going deeper into layers of hurt and violence, sometimes as perpetrator, sometimes as victim, that had been part of his life for nearly 40 years. I sat alongside Simon, listening as he shared his pain. He shed tears, I assured him of God's love and forgiveness. As Simon returned to his cell, I knew the guilt and shame he now carried was less and the

---

[12] Neil Ormerod, 'Reconciliation and the Paschal Mystery,' in *A Hunger for Reconciliation*, Gerard Moore (ed.) (NSW: St Pauls, 2004), 52.

peace and forgiveness he feels had increased. And I had come to a profound understanding of the words of Jesus: 'Whatever you loose on earth will be loosed in heaven, and whatever you bind on earth will be bound in heaven.' Each of us has the power to forgive sins. And the power to retain sins, keeping either ourselves or the other bound. This choice is ours.[13]

Forgiveness is an act of faith, trusting that God's mercy is greater than one's sins. The task of the pastoral carer is to lead others to the assurance of God's forgiveness and the release from guilt.

Sacrament of Marriage

Marriage is the precursor to family life. It is a thanksgiving and commitment for the future and a desire to deepen a couple's relationship. The sacrament of marriage blesses the intimate relationship that involves physical, social, emotional and spiritual dimensions. The vows make it clear that commitment in marriage is commitment to the other, 'For better, for worse,' whatever the quality of relationship or the circumstances over a long period. 'Till death do us part' means pastoral care of each other is ongoing, through thick and thin. It is about sustaining a loving relationship over a life-time and in difficult times.

Sacrament of Ordination

The Sacrament of Holy Order is a charismatic gift for the benefit of all. Those who are ordained to the priesthood are to work as disciples of Christ, to lead in the ministries of preaching, celebrating sacraments, and enabling the gifts of all to work with 'holy order'.

A priest's pastoral and sacramental role are vital, yet the primary task of the priest is to form a parish which is about a community, gathered to share and grow from one another. A contemporary understanding of the ordained is seen in the following by Reverend Bill Loader:[14]

> We have ordained you to the Ministry of the Word . . .
> The bread is on the table. You need to break it and ensure it is distributed. The cup is already poured. You need to ensure

---

[13] Elizabeth Lee, 'Prison Ministry has Changed Me' in *Eremos* Sept 2014, No 128, p. 19.
[14] Bill Loader, *Ordination charge*
http://wwwstaff.murdoch.edu.au/~loader/charge.html

its celebration is shared. Brokenness in compassion is not to be confused with our failures in stress management; the poured out life is not to be confused with burn out. You are not called to be the saviour of the world, but to pass the bread and the wine. The miracle is not how far you can stretch yourself, but how faithfully you lay the table. The decorations of pious language and the sentiments of specific cultures are not the meal. Art and beauty may point to it, but the true art and beauty is the vision of reconciliation which that meal prefigures and the life of lowly service it re-presents . . .

What the world needs most is Jesus and the elements are all there. Feed richly and feed others richly. Lead people out and lead people in; lead people to the places of bread and wine.

We have not ordained you to ministry; that happened at your baptism...

We have not ordained you to be a caring person; you are already called to that . . .

We have ordained you to something smaller and less spectacular: to read and interpret those sacred stories of our community so that they speak the Word to people today;

to remember and practise those rituals and rites of meaning which in their poetry address people at the level where change operates;

to foster in community through Word and Sacrament and pastoral care that encounter with truth which will set people free to minister as the body of Christ.

We have ordained you to the Ministry of the Word. Amen.

Sacrament of Anointing of the sick

The Rite of Anointing of the sick is a sacrament offered to the chronically ill, aged, infirm and those undergoing surgery.

Are any among you suffering? They should pray. Are any cheerful? They should sing songs of praise. Are any among you sick? They should call for the elders of the church and have them pray over them, anointing them with oil in the name of the Lord. The prayer of faith will save the sick, and the Lord will raise them up; and anyone who has committed sins will be forgiven. - **James 5:13-15**

The practice of anointing of the sick includes the pastoral ministry of counsel, prayer, reading the Scriptures, bringing communion and listening to confessions, in order to restore people to spiritual, physical and psychological health. The sacramental encounter with God, allows one to find meaning in suffering, and hope for eternal life.

God offers the anointed person grace to overcome anxiety, find comfort, to be healed and become whole. All those who gather around the bed of the ailing, participate in the ceremony as a sign of their concern.

Sacramentals

Sacramental objects are holy objects, laden with divine power. For Catholic congregations, candles, medals, rosary beads, pictures or statues of Jesus, Mary and the saints serve as sacramentals, where the transcendent is perceived to be present. Benedictions, anointing oil over bodies, sprinkling holy water around the home and on people, are important and are 'points of contact' between God and the person, are symbolic in nature and contribute to sanctifying various occasions in human life.

Reflection

They had been hand picked
Chosen to follow Jesus as disciples.
They had watched, observed, questioned, learnt.
Then Jesus was gone.
The memory could have stayed fondly in their hearts
But is reminiscing enough when you have caught fire?
That Pentecost day it all erupted.
God's Holy Spirit was suddenly there,
Was probably always there,
Since the hovering over the waters of Creation,
And when Jesus told them repeatedly,
'I am in my Father, and you in me, and I in you' (John 14:20).
But now the disciples were awakened to this presence.
Sudden illumination of minds, burning of hearts,
Awareness had set in. God was there all along.
No longer disciples now, but impelled to action.
To become Apostles,
for God's Spirit is here and there and everywhere
Calling, stirring, inviting, encouraging.
To now be Christ, as Christ was,
To leave this place, to go out there,
Encounter, invite, accept, renew,
To awaken the world to the presence of God's
Holy Spirit here and now
And so come to know hope, experience comfort and find love.
Amen.

Chapter 3: Models of pastoral care today

> Again, we may think of ourselves as reaching out to others, bringing compassion and godly enlightenment. If so, we cast them as recipients, ourselves as donors, and God as operating through us to them. Of course, God may do this. But, alternatively, we could think of ourselves as reaching out to others who are already embraced and touched by God. If so, we cast them as donors, ourselves as recipients, and God as operating through them to us. Then we will be amazed at God's versatility! But we can be both donor and recipient, bearer of God and receiver of God. Then we will be truly committed to the ministry that characterised Jesus, who not only brought healing love to others, but who was frequently edified, nourished, by the faith and grace he encountered in them. - **Anthony J. Gittins**[15]

Jesus as our pastoral care model

If our model for pastoral care comes from Jesus, who called himself the Good Shepherd (John 10), then caring takes on numerous forms as we read in the Gospels. Jesus' care extended to one and all: Jews and Gentiles, females and males, young and old. Jesus expressed his care for people's physical, spiritual and emotional state. His care was not limited to cures but included being outspoken on issues concerning the voiceless. Ways Jesus demonstrated concern and care for others include:

- Defending those who couldn't save themselves, such as the woman caught in adultery (John 8:1-11)
- Blessing others as Jesus blesses the children (Mark 10:13-16)
- Healing and restoring to wholeness, as Jesus did through miraculous healings and exorcisms
- Teaching and educating as Jesus did through parables

---

[15] Anthony J. Gittins *Reading the Clouds. Mission Spirituality for New Times*, (Strathfield: St Pauls, 1999), 131.

- Providing basic necessities as Jesus did through feeding the 5000 (Matthew 14:13-21)
- Comforting the grieving as Jesus did with the woman from Nain (Luke 7:11-17)
- Offering hope as the resurrected Jesus did to the disciples (Luke 24:44-49)
- Restoring to life what was dormant as Jesus did with Jairus' daughter (Luke 8:49-56) and Lazarus (John 11:38-44)
- Empowering others as Jesus did with the mission of the 70 (Luke 10:38-42)
- Praying with others as when Jesus taught the Lord's prayer (Luke 10:1-4)
- Being outspoken on justice issues, as Jesus exhorted to fearless confession (Luke 12:4-12)
- Advocating for the vulnerable as he did for the woman who was a sinner (Luke 7:36-50)

Types of pastoral care

In earlier times, the view was taken that pastoral care must aim at conversion, leading the person more fully and explicitly into the life of faith and the Church. In this view, pastoral care is understood primarily as evangelisation. However, this sort of care of bringing the Gospel to people, has generally been superseded to allowing the Gospel to lead one to people.

> The Church today is challenged to abandon the crusading spirit of the Enlightenment paradigm with its arrogant superiority complex, naïve optimism, and pragmatic activism, and to pursue its mission of witnessing to Christ in a more humble, contemplative and dialogic key – **Fr Michael McCabe**[16]

---

[16] Quoted by Noel Connolly in 'A great welcome for ourselves' https://www.columban.org.au/media-and-publications/newsletters-and-bulletins/columban-ebulletin/archive/2016/e-news-vol.9-no.6/fr-noel-connolly-a-great-welcome-for-ourselves?quip_thread=article15410&quip_parent=1123

We need to give up our 'crusading minds' and 'teacher complexes' and take on a 'crucified mind' – being present to and suffering with others – **Noel Connolly and Kosuke Koyama**[17]
Effective Christian witness is not about bombarding people with religious messages, but about our willingness to be available to others - **Pope Francis**[18]

Although pastoral care today is not so much focused on bringing the Gospel to others for conversion but rather more about being present and attentive to others, Andrew Purves argues that - without explicit grounding in Jesus, an explicit sharing in his life and ministry - pastoral work accommodates itself to ideologies or theisms, becoming a cultural expression of care, but bereft of the truth and power of the gospel.[19]

So how does one get involved with a patient's moral dilemma without, on the one hand, agreeing with everything they say, or on the other, imposing one's views? What follows is an insight into how even a great theologian such as Karl Rahner experiences doubt as he undertakes home visitations:

> O God, these people to whom you've thrown me out from my home with you! Mostly they won't accept me, your messenger, at all; they want nothing to do with your gifts, your grace, and your truth, with which you have sent me to them . . . And as for those who do let me in their houses that are their lives! They normally want anything but what I am meant to be bringing from you. They want to tell me about their wretched, tiny concerns; they want to pour out their hearts to me . . . And what do these people want of me? If it is not simply money, material help, or a little comfort from a sympathetic heart that they're seeking, they mostly look on me as some kind of insurance agent, with

---

[17] Noel Connolly referencing Kosuke Koyama in 'A great welcome for ourselves'
https://www.columban.org.au/media-and-publications/newsletters-and-bulletins/columban-ebulletin/archive/2016/e-news-vol.9-no.6/fr-noel-connolly-a-great-welcome-for-ourselves?quip_thread=article15410&quip_parent=1123

[18] Message of Pope Francis for The 48th World Communications Day
Communication at the Service of an Authentic Culture of Encounter [Sunday, 1 June 2014]
https://w2.vatican.va/content/francesco/en/messages/communications/documents/papa-francesco_20140124_messaggio-comunicazioni-sociali.html

[19] Andrew Purves, *Reconstructing Pastoral Theology. A Christological Foundation*, (Louisville: Westminster John Knox Press, 2004), 179.

whom they can take out a heavenly accident policy to prevent your breaking in upon their lives in the omnipotence of your holiness and justice, shaking them out of their tiny everyday concerns and their narrow Sunday self-satisfaction . . . How rarely does anyone want to confront the gift of your grace as it really is: tough, clear, not just for our consolation but also your glory, pure and upright, silent and bold.[20]

Karl Rahner asks the question, 'Am I the sort of messenger who just hands over your message and gift at the "delivery entrance", without ever being allowed to enter into the "interior castle" of another's soul so as to be able to make sure that your message and your gift really becomes eternal life for this person through this person's free love?' Rahner concludes, 'All care of souls – in its ultimate, true reality – is possible only in you, in your love that binds me to you and thus takes me with it also to the place to which you alone can still find a way: to human hearts'.[21]

The question of how to care pastorally and what makes care a Catholic practice has been debated over time. Frank Lopez raises some issues as to what makes pastoral care distinct:[22]

- If it is to be called pastoral care, must it be directly concerned with a person's religious faith?
- Is it the motivation arising from the carer's faith in Christ and the transcendent dimension within the context of caring, even if it is only implicit, that makes an act of caring one of pastoral care?
- If it is to be pastoral care, must the carer be a designated person acting on behalf of the Church?

According to Lopez, pastoral care is a ministry that involves our humanness/createdness and not just religious beliefs. It is a service that is personal, caring and compassionate. Thus pastoral care today places emphasis on meeting each person's needs, rather than the carer having a pre-determined agenda. This model stresses the characteristics of the pastoral relationship as non-judgmental, empathic, supportive and

---

[20] Karl Rahner, 'God of my Sisters and Brothers,' in *Karl Rahner. Spiritual Writings*. Edited by Philip Endean, (Maryknoll: Orbis Books, 2004), 107-108.
[21] Rahner, 'God of my Sisters and Brothers,' 109-110.
[22] Frank Lopez, *Applied Pastoral Care: A Contextual Approach*, (Hunters Hill: Marist Centre for Pastoral Care, 1995).

working towards getting the person to take greater self-responsibility. Yet it still remains a ministry that arises from the conviction of faith within the carer to be a witness to Jesus' love for all people.

The question of what constitutes pastoral care today comes up against another stark reality that far fewer people now express their spirituality through participation in the rituals. Pastoral care today needs to be self-aware, open to the experiences of others, and able to articulate a theology that is of practical relevance as Christopher Swift identifies.[23] As such, pastoral care takes on different shapes and practices that have incorporated the contexts of the times.

Three Models of Pastoral Care

The process of discerning God's 'heart and mind' and putting Christian beliefs into practice in changing circumstances involves Scripture, understanding of Tradition, and personal experience. At least three distinct models of pastoral care have emerged according to Elaine Graham:[24]

- Therapeutic
- Classical/Missionary
- Liberation

Fresh understandings of faith, resulting from contemporary theology, social sciences, such as psychology, and organisational theories of leadership and management, have influenced and altered the practice of pastoral care.

Therapeutic model

Popularised forms of Christian care are modelled on the dynamics of therapeutic practice, and advanced perspectives on human personality founded on psychology and theology.[25]

---

[23] Christopher Swift, *Hospital Chaplaincy in the Twenty-first Century*, (England: Ashgate, 2009), 135, 144.
[24] Elaine Graham, *Words made Flesh: Writings in Pastoral and Practical Theology*, (SCM Press: London, 2009).
[25] Elaine Graham, *Words made Flesh: Writings in Pastoral and Practical Theology*, (SCM Press: London, 2009), 138. The 'religion and health' movement grew from here, bringing together psychiatrists, physicians, clergy, theologians and health care chaplains. Leading figures include Seward Hiltner, Hannah Tillich, Eric Erikson, Rollo May and Carl Rogers.

Psychotherapy and religion are the two major sources of modern individual identity formation, providing concepts and technologies for ordering the interior life, strategies of personal salvation and establishing a deep structure for understanding life. They propose matters of ultimate importance and contours of an ethical system for making decisions about one's life.[26]

Elaine Graham explains that a therapeutic model of Church emphasises as its key activity the practice of personal care, support and healing. The primary locus of such a model is upon the interpersonal encounter, the intimacies of listening, conversation and solicitous concern. The theological dimensions lie in the emphasis on the implicit values of healing, reconciliation and justice for individuals and communities.[27]

Criticism of the therapeutic model include:

- In applying the therapeutic model, one needs to be aware of an over commitment to crisis ministry, and to curative and pathological patterns, at the expense of preventative or developmental interventions.[28]

- It becomes so assimilated into the secular humanist world-view that it abandons any distinctive Christian perspective. The danger lies in the uncritical adoption of presuppositions and practices without the contribution of theological critique.[29]

However, the model is not an abandonment of theological values. It is discerning the signs of the times within therapeutic movements, and their best insights, for the renewal of pastoral care. The freedom of the client to find paths of growth and forgiveness via the therapeutic relationship, appears to resonate with Christian values, while articulating them in terms accessible to modern culture.[30]

---

[26]David G. Benner, *Care of Souls. Revisioning Christian Nurture and Counsel*, (Grand Rapids, Michigan: Baker Books, 1998), 44.
[27]Elaine L. Graham, *Words made flesh. Writings in pastoral and practical Theology*, (London: SCM Press, 2009), 148.
[28]Graham, Elaine, *Words made Flesh: Writings in Pastoral and Practical Theology*, (SCM Press: London, 2009), 141.
[29]Emmanuel Y. Lartey, *Pastoral Theology in an Intercultural World* (Cleveland, Ohio: The Pilgrim Press, 2006), 81.
[30]Graham, Elaine, *Words made Flesh: Writings in Pastoral and Practical Theology*, (SCM Press: London, 2009), 140.

Paul Tillich argued that modern psychologies enabled contemporary culture to explore and articulate deep anxieties and existential problems to which theology could respond with renewed clarity and purpose. Yet psychology can never deduce either meaning or morality from its scientific or descriptive activities. Similarly, theology is not well equipped to render personality dynamics intelligible, and yet it offers a perspective on life that only becomes meaningful when it is embedded in the core of a person's psycho-spiritual functioning. Each needs the other.[31] As Richard Rohr explains, after the early stages of identity and belonging are worked through, real transformation does not seem to take place apart from some kind of contact with the Transcendent or Absolute. Therapeutic healing will always be the effect, but it is the relationship to the Transcendent that matters.[32]

The Classical/Missionary model

The classical/missionary model reflects values of community or fellowship *(koinonia)* and self-emptying (kenosis) as its centre. It is the presence of the Church in the world as the tangible expression of God's grace.[33]

The Church delivers a range of care offered by members of a congregation which includes visiting the sick, attending to the dying, comforting the bereaved, supporting those who are facing difficulties, preaching, and administering the sacraments.

The strength of the classical/missionary model lies in its rooting of pastoral action within the life of the Christian community and the collective ministry of the congregation. Furthermore, it concentrates on activities of formation and vocation, and not simply on curing and healing that the therapeutic model tends to.

However, the classical/missionary model restricts its sources and norms too closely to the received wisdom of the Church tradition. Any model of pastoral action must include not just ecclesiastical imperatives but the eschatological call as well. The life of communities

---

[31]David G. Benner, *Care of Souls. Revisioning Christian Nurture and Counsel*, (Grand Rapids, Michigan: Baker Books, 1998), 69.
[32]Richard Rohr, *What the mystics know. Seven pathways to your deeper self*, (New York: The Crossroad Publishing company, 2015), 139.
[33]Graham, Elaine, *Words made Flesh: Writings in Pastoral and Practical Theology*, (SCM Press: London, 2009), 149.

that proclaim and embody such values must be gathered and outward-looking; faithful and prophetic.[34]

The Second Vatican Council understood the Church to be more than just the inclusion into a strictly sacramental life. Its mission to care extends into the world as the universal Body of Christ.

In Matthew 12:14-21, we read a description about Jesus as fulfilling God's purposes and activities in the world. It was 'justice to the Gentiles' (Matthew 12:18), and not just to the Jews. Furthermore, 'He will not wrangle or cry aloud, nor will anyone hear his voice in the streets' (Matthew 12:19). Justice will be served by care, attention to the least, 'He will not break a bruised reed or quench a smouldering wick' (Matthew 12:20). Justice and hope prevail when one attends to the role of nurturing, protecting, encouraging and gently caring for the most vulnerable. However, justice and care has found other ways of expression in modern times including gaining justice through signing petitions, lobbying the governments, street marches, court battles, etc. This brings us to the next model.

The Liberation Model

Latin American theologians argue that faithful action necessitates a 'preferential option for the poor.' The liberation model has theology as orthopraxis in which the truth of the gospel is measured by its ability to bring life, right relation, justice and full humanity into the world.

The Liberation model engages communities to participate in God's kingdom and follow the lead of the Spirit. The objectives of pastoral activity as Elaine Graham notes, are social transformation, action for justice, liberation in the public and political domain, in medical and welfare institutions, via social policy measures, political intervention or community development. Salvation embraces the entire inhabited universe.[35] As Gustavo Gutierrez writes:

> . . . to struggle against misery and exploitation and to build a just society is already to be part of the saving action which is moving towards the complete fulfilment . . . This dimension of the preaching of the gospel, which rejects any aseptic presentation of the message, should lead to a profound revision

---

[34]Graham, *Words made Flesh: Writings in Pastoral and Practical Theology*, 144-145.
[35]Graham, *Words made Flesh: Writings in Pastoral and Practical Theology*, 149.

of the pastoral activity of the Church. Thus this activity should be addressed effectively and primarily to those who are oppressed . . . or better still, the oppressed themselves should be the agents of their own pastoral activity.[36]

The person exercising pastoral care aims at creating conditions or offering services which help others liberate themselves from limiting circumstances and to enable them to develop and achieve their full potential as mature persons.

In his encyclical *Evangelii Gaudium*, Pope Francis offers important insights into ministering to others including: 'Face-to-face encounter with others, with their physical presence which challenges us' (EG 88) and the invitation to draw near to forms of poverty and vulnerability (EG 210).

In the Canaanite woman account (Matthew 15:21-28), the message is that all people have the right to liberating care. She is a non-Jew and non-Israelite (from Tyre and Sidon). She has no claim on Jesus, who was a male, a Jew, and a resident of Israel. Yet she ignores culture and creed, gender and nationality, to demand and plead her daughter's cause and Jesus approves her request. The Gospel challenge is to open minds, widen understanding and broaden views to see every person as worthy of attention. To believe that it is our responsibility to attend the needs of all, no matter who they are or where they come from. Human rights equity, power, autonomy, and the dignity of persons matter. Christian faith and pastoral work call into focus the eschatological imperative to anticipate, through action, the coming of God's kingdom.

Yet the criticisms of liberation theology include that an interventionist and preventative stance isn't always adopted and justice, structures, and power dynamics need to be addressed. All too often, the adoption of liberation theology is a call to politicise the Church instead. There is also the tendency to campaign on behalf of the poor rather than empowering them. Furthermore, there is a need to resist the doctrines of progress and emancipation that undervalue the task of helping one another to live well and truthfully within situations where there are no cures and answers. This is termed 'sustaining,' which is distinguished from 'curing.' Humanity may be partners in God's

---

[36]Gustavo Gutierrez, *A Theology of Liberation (Maryknoll, New York: Orbis*, 1973), 159, 270-271.

redemptive activity, but ultimately, human healing and salvation are gifts of God, contingent upon grace.[37]

As Richard Rohr notes, there are those who give out bread instead of the word of God, perhaps out of a sense of guilt or a need to feel effective. Perhaps they doubt that they have anything to give in Christ. Perhaps they don't know that they have anything to give in praying with a person, giving a person hope or love. Sometimes basic necessities are important but this shouldn't be used as an excuse to avoid the power of God's liberation of the self.[38]

A definition of pastoral care

Reflecting on the three models of pastoral care, one can describe the concerns of pastoral care as involving:
- the pursuit of human wholeness
- the actions of the Church in the world
- the realisation of justice and equity

There is a gradual shifting of focus in pastoral care:[39]
- From a sacramental focus to placing more attention to evangelisation and humanisation
- From working autonomously, to learning to work as a team member in a communal spirit
- To be concerned about promoting life, from its beginning to its natural end
- Witnessing to the ministry of compassion, combined with being more outspoken on issues related to ethics and justice
- Ministering from a religious paradigm but also learning to care in open, ecumenical and intercultural perspectives

Pastoral care is a ministry of compassionate presence, modelled on Jesus' care for people, especially those hurting and in need. It seeks to empower growth toward wholeness, renewing and enriching one's

---

[37] Graham, *Words made Flesh: Writings in Pastoral and Practical Theology*, 148.
[38] Richard Rohr, *What the mystics know. Seven pathways to your deeper self*, (New York: The Crossroad Publishing company, 2015), 128-129.
[39] Arnaldo Pangrazzi, *The Art of Caring for the sick. Guidelines for Creative Ministry*, (NY: St Pauls, 2013), 53.

relationship with God and others, and equipping people to better live in the world. So, definitions of pastoral care today include:

Helping acts, done by representative Christian persons, directed towards healing, sustaining, guiding, and reconciling of troubled persons whose troubles arise in the context of ultimate meanings and concerns - **William A. Clebsch and Charles R. Jaekle (1964)**

Pastoral care is a person-centred, holistic approach to care that complements the care offered by other helping disciplines while paying particular attention to spiritual care. The focus of pastoral care is upon the healing, guiding, supporting, reconciling, nurturing, liberating, and empowering of people in whatever situation they find themselves - **Bruce Rumbold, La Trobe University School of Public Health** http://pastoralcareact.org/pastoral.html

Pastoral care is informed by authoritative sources in Scripture and in Christian tradition, by the resources of social sciences and personal experiences and finally reason. It has both a restorative and transformative intent. Aside from pastoral care, there is spiritual care, theological care (Doehring, 2004) and soul care (Anderson, 2001), which are other descriptors now proposed in ministries to people who face crises, traumas, loss or personal dilemmas.

Reflection

*There are no excuses to deny the call to give of ourselves,
for the way we offer care can be varied.
We could cook for others if we are a Master Chef
We could sit and listen to stories if we have time
We could draw up petitions if a legislation threatens
We could raise funds to purchase much needed resources
We could tell amusing tales to ease a burdened mind
We could hold a hand that trembles with fear
We could be a guiding light to someone lost in doubt
We could fix a few things for someone who can't
We could become foster carers if we have room
We could advocate for change if we had clout
We could be a shoulder for others to cry on
We could sing a lullaby to one needing sleep
We could be a person who cares, if we want to. Amen.*

Chapter 4: Do we really care anyway?

> The totally human, human being, the poets enable us to see, is the one who weeps over evil, revels in goodness, loves outrageously, and carries the pain of the world in healing hands. Feeling is the mark of saints. It is Vincent de Paul tending the poor on the back streets of France, Mother Teresa with a dying beggar in her arms, Florence Nightingale tending the wounded in the midst of battle, John the apostle resting trustingly on the breast of Jesus, Damian binding the running sores of lepers on the island of Molokai, the soup-kitchen people in our own towns giving hours of their lives, week after fruitless week, to feed the undernourished children, the homeless women, and the down-and-outs. Feeling, we know deep within us, signals the real measure of a soul. - **Joan D. Chittister**[40]

When we talk about caring, we assume it is an innate ability in all of us, as created in God's image. However, is that the case? It is worth asking and has been debated. William Golding's novel *Lord of the flies* depicts a downward spiral of behaviour when school boys stranded on an island move from civility and reason to the savage survivalism of primeval hunters. Three boys are left dead by the end of the novel.

Only recently, Florida teens recorded a drowning man and did nothing to assist him. The report is below and makes us question people's ability to empathise, to care, to love.

> A group of Florida teens who taunted a drowning man while filming his death from afar will not be criminally charged, according to police.
>
> In the more than two-minute long video, the five teen boys - who are between the ages of 14 and 16 - can be heard laughing as the man struggles to stay afloat, police say, in a pond near his family's Cocoa, Florida, home.
>
> Instead of calling for help, the teens recorded the incident on a cell phone, chuckling during the victim's final moments.

---

[40] Joan D. Chittister, *Heart of Flesh*, (Grand Rapids, Michigan: Wm B Eerdmans Pub, 1998), 50

The teens can be heard warning the man that he was 'going to die' and they were not going to help him. At one point, one of the teen boys can be heard laughing, saying 'he dead.'

Police say the incident happened on July 9, but even after the teens recorded the video and witnessed the man drown, they did nothing to alert authorities.

'At least one of the teens expressed no remorse while being interviewed by detectives,' Martinez said, claiming the fact that they did not report the incident to authorities further speaks to their lack of remorse.

The family of the victim, identified as 31-year-old Jamel Dunn, initially filed a missing person's report on July 12, three days after he had already drowned.

His body was recovered from the water on July 14.

... 'As law enforcement officers, we are sworn to uphold and enforce the laws,' he said. 'Unfortunately, there are no laws in Florida that apply to this scenario. Perhaps this case may be what's needed to pass new laws.'

'As chief of police, there are times when I wish I could do more. But I'm a firm believer in that good will always win over evil,' he added. 'It may not come in our lifetime, but there will be justice.'

The teens were interviewed by police, during which they admitted to being in the area 'smoking weed,' police said.

Their identities have not been released because they are juveniles who committed no crime, police say. But the nature of the incident has troubled even the most seasoned law enforcement officials.

'I've been doing this a long time, probably 20 years or more ... I was horrified. My jaw dropped,' Martinez said.

'To think that anyone would just lack any kind of moral conscience to call for help,' Martinez said. 'It's one thing to see something and not want to put yourself at risk, but to not call anybody, to sit there and to laugh and humiliate this person is beyond my comprehension.'

'I feel like something should be done to (the teens),' Dunn's sister said in a Facebook Live video she posted on Thursday. 'I don't care if it's probation or something, it just needs to be an eye-opener. A lesson learned.'

'If they can sit there and watch somebody die in front of their eyes, imagine what they're going to do when they get older. Where's the morals?' she asked.[41]

So does care come naturally to humans? In the parable of the Good Samaritan (Luke 10:29-37), one may think otherwise. A beaten man lies dying on a road. 'By chance' some people pass along and ignore the injuries of the person in desperate need of safety and care. The Priest and Levite saw 'trouble' while the Samaritan saw 'chance' at helping the dying man. We are meant to be more than 'passers-by.' We are meant to have eyes to see, ears to hear and hearts moved with compassion.

The Good Samaritan then offers pastoral care. He notes the situation, stops and takes time out for the person in need. Yet more than just offering aid, the Good Samaritan 'was moved with pity' having a deep gut reaction to the injured man (Luke 10:33). Through empathy, the Good Samaritan was determined to improve the fortune of the person. The Samaritan's mercy, risk, generosity and practical attention to the needs of the afflicted, indicate God's concern for those whom others despise.

Today, there exists in some places what is termed 'The Good Samaritan Law':

> A good samaritan in legal terms refers to someone who renders aid in an emergency to an injured person on a voluntary basis. Usually, if a volunteer comes to the aid of an injured or ill person who is a stranger, the person giving the aid owes the stranger a duty of being reasonably careful. A person is not obligated by law to do first aid in most states, not unless it's part of a job description. However, some states will consider it an act of negligence, though, if a person doesn't at least call for help. Generally, where an unconscious victim cannot respond, a good

---

[41] Nick Valencia and Devon Sayers, 'Florida teens who recorded drowning man will not be charged in his death' - CNN.*com* July 21st, 2017 http://edition.cnn.com/2017/07/20/us/florida-teens-drowning-man/index.html

samaritan can help them on the grounds of implied consent. However, if the victim is conscious and can respond, a person should ask their permission to help them first.

Some states offer immunity to good samaritans, but sometimes negligence could result in a claim of negligent care if the injuries or illness were made worse by the volunteer's negligence. Statutes typically don't exempt a good samaritan who acts in a wilful and wanton or reckless manner in providing the care, advice, or assistance.[42]

What is meant to be care has now become legislated and risks a legal court case if the care administered is not appropriate. One wonders why there is reservation in offering care. Jesus himself faced downright resistance and opposition to any hint of mercy and compassion, care and generosity.

- Jesus was rejected in his home town of Nazareth when he dared declare he has come to offer justice (Luke 4:29)
- Jesus heals a paralytic and all the scribes could do was question his authority (Mark 2:1-12)
- He was criticised when his disciples plucked heads of grain to appease their hunger (Luke 6:1-5)
- Jesus heals a man with a withered hand (Mark 3:1-6, Luke 6:6-11) and a man with dropsy (Luke 14:1-6) on the Sabbath and so earns the fury of the religious leaders
- Pharisees rigorously investigate the healing of a blind man by Jesus (John 9:13-34)
- Heals a Gerasene Demoniac and was cast out by the villagers (Luke 8:35-37)
- Mocked by Jairus and his wife when he promised to raise their daughter (Luke 8:52-53)
- Jesus was accused of being in league with Beelzebul after performing healings (Mark 3:22-27, Luke 11:14-16)
- Jesus' authority was questioned (Luke 20:1-8)

---

[42] 'Good Samaritans law and Legal Definition.' https://definitions.uslegal.com/g/good-samaritans/

However, Jesus did not remain silent and refuse to concede to the pressure, criticism and ongoing threats. He challenged the mindsets that would silence good by denouncing the Pharisees and Lawyers (Luke 11:37-52) and Scribes (Mark 12:38-40, Luke 20:45-47).

So do we need laws to tell us to care for others? Is it suggesting humans are less likely to offer care, if it is not legislated? To all evidence it appears so, as we see now with mandatory reporting of child neglect or abuse, which is ever so prevalent.

Then there is the proliferation of virtual reality games where violence, blood and gore, shooting and killing are the draw cards for socially accepted entertainment.

The *Avengers* and *Justice League* comic franchise are now block buster movies with their lust for world scale weaponry, fight scenes on a grand scale, and where muscle power, brute force and alluring beauty earn admiration. And, of course, there is history with its legacy of battles and wars, century after century.

To care seems to be something that is either not innate in us or lies dormant. People need to be taught how to care, what it means to empathise with another. But how can that be when we live in a society that focuses on fame, power, beauty and fortune? We have become numb to pain, blinded to suffering, sanitised from disease, oblivious to evil, ignorant of reality, devoid of any sense of responsibility towards others. In this postmodern era, suffering is defined as evil, such that now one's every need must be met, and it's all about the individual and their pleasures.

We don't need to create robots for we have become machines that simply do the bidding of corporate giants. We pop their pills, we are complicit to their wrong doings, we are silenced by money, we demonise what takes us out of our comfort zone, we place riches and beauty on a pedestal, we purchase our happiness and consume arrogance, and don't believe there is anything else worthy of our attention.

Maggie Hamilton sees the problem lying in the fact that we now live in a performance culture, where boys and girls are expected to be amazing due to consumer capitalism, mass media and popular culture. This cradle to grave marketing knows that for every brand that captures a child, they become worth $100,000 to that brand, for life.

She goes on to note that what is being observed in children today is:[43]
- a massive rise in anxiety
- concern about looks/body image
- they believe in the message, 'I am what I own' so that possessions count most
- no longer playing imaginative play, but instead follow scripts they have heard from ads, video games, reality TV, media and pop culture on how to be. These scripts 'are getting more risqué, and are giving our children lots of cues for how they should be behaving in ways that are really disturbing.'
- very vulnerable to suggestions by media
- remaining at the immature stage, because young people are not having life experiences. They are stuck in a 'just about me and having everything now' attitude
- very little inner life as they are exposed to shallow messages

Hamilton says corporations take the anxieties of children, and their aspirations, and sell them back to them as products.[44]

Then there is also the premature sexualisation of children, especially girls, with adultified tweens and growth in child trafficking. There is the ever-growing incidence of bullying and sexual harassment in schoolyards and more insidiously, in cyberspace. Games on the internet include stripping girls, peering up a teacher's skirt, gang rape of drunk girls, all which impact on behaviour. *Grand theft* auto game has killing of prostitutes and police, which patterns boys to be violent. And we ask why there is an absence of care!

Young people idolise the likes of Lady Gaga, whose embodiment of 'the new sexy' is a disturbing aspect. At a concert in Australia, she came down a rope dripping in blood and in a music clip, she simulates gang rape. Porn now rivals sport in the field where most money is made.

---

[43]Maggie Hamilton, 'What's happening to our boys and girls?' at *Happiness & Its Causes 2011 Conference.*
https://www.youtube.com/watch?v=6T8QIiU09pc
[44]ibid

According to Maggie Hamilton, living in such a toxic and dysfunctional environment is taking its toll on the mind, body and spirit of our young people, undermining their growth and happiness. Hamilton states that we need to reclaim public spaces that have been invaded by advertisements that promote toxic messages. She notes 'Our kids are not the problem. They reflect back to us our values.' This is a real eye opener for adults. What do we really want to teach children?

In such an all pervasive and toxic environment for young and old alike, it becomes very difficult to foster good choices, clear consciences and honest hearts in people. So in order grow our children body, mind and spirit, they need to connect to the world directly, having a childhood earlier generations had. Basically, it still takes a village to raise our children as Maggie Hamilton concludes.

The absence of care is nothing new. In the Scriptures, from the outset we read of Cain's murder of his brother Abel. When God questions Cain, his response is, 'Am I my brother's keep?' (Genesis 4:9). Yes, you are. We all are. Each one of us is the keeper of those around us. Even if responsibility is shirked, accountability ignored, rights abused, ultimately the actions or lack thereof, will judge us. We cannot escape ourselves! As Cain learnt with horror that would torment him all his life, 'My punishment is greater than I can bear' (Genesis 4:13). Perhaps that is why war veterans experience trauma years on.

It is our innate ability to care, to be moved by the plight of others. However, whether we act on it is another matter. Whatever our sins, they will remain. Life ultimately makes its rightful claim on us. We will have to face the truth of ourselves.

Those who open themselves to humanity with compassion are those who become less afraid of life and more courageous in giving of themselves. Those who close in on themselves refuse to engage with the world's needs. We need to choose constantly. Do we choose to become our 'brother's keeper' or not? The consequences of our choices are manifold and determine whether good or bad triumphs.

When Jesus accepts the invitation to a meal at Martha and Mary's home, he says the powerful words, 'Mary has chosen the better part, which will not be taken away from her' (Luke 10:42). Her choice . . . to be with the other, to offer her presence, hospitality, her care and love. It is to people such as these that the world owes much. They build, they create, they encourage, they pave the way for a better future for others. So what do we choose?

Today, according to Sharon Brous,[45] a shared religious ethos is emerging in the form of revitalised religion. The first is wakefulness. We live in a time of unprecedented access to information about every global tragedy that happens. Psychologists tell us that the more we learn about what's broken in our world, the less likely we are to do anything. It's called psychic numbing. It's our job to pull people out of their apathy and into the anguish, and insist that we do what we don't want to do and see what we do not want to see.

The second principle is hope. It may be the single greatest act of defiance against a politics of pessimism and against a culture of despair. Religion is supposed to be about giving people back a sense of purpose, a sense of hope, a sense that they and their dreams fundamentally matter in this world that tells them that they don't matter.

The third principle is mightiness. Religious communities and ritual can remind us, whatever gifts, blessings and resources we have, we must use them to make the world a bit more just and loving. It is worth reiterating here, 'it takes a village to raise a child'.

The fourth is interconnectedness. A few years ago, a man was walking on the beach in Alaska when he came across a soccer ball that had some Japanese letters written on it. He took a picture of it and posted it on social media, and a Japanese teenager contacted him. He had lost everything in the tsunami that devastated his country, but he was able to retrieve that soccer ball after it had floated all the way across the Pacific. We are all in this together. Religion can and must be a force for good in the world, a shift toward love, justice, equality and dignity for all.[46]

---

[45]Sharon Brous: It's time to reclaim religion. TEDWomen 2016 · Filmed October 2016 · 16:27 http://www.ted.com/talks/sharon_brous_it_s_time_to_reclaim_and_reinvent_religion/transcript?language=en
[46]ibid.

Reflection

What makes me the better I?
It can't be more possessions for then those who have none
would never achieve their I.
It can't be beauty, fame or fortune, for so many have these
and haven't fulfilled their I.
What makes me the better I?
It comes from within,
That inner peace
That person deep in my recesses
That is willing to give
Is made to love
That freely accepts all
That gently cares.
I am
When I love.
I am better
When I nourish relationships.
I am who I am
When I allow my humanity to shine
When I can hear the cry of the world
When I can shed tears of empathy
When I am moved with compassion
When I lend a helping hand
When I look with love
When I speak words of hope
When I truly care.
Then I am fully human
Then I am the better I. Amen.

Chapter 5: Qualities of a pastoral carer

> Week after week, Christ washes the disciples' dirty feet, handles their very toes, and repeats, it is all right - believe it or not - to be people. - **Annie Dillard**[47]
>
> We are all created frail and vulnerable in our bodies, storm-tossed in our emotions and limited in our understanding – **Sheila Cassidy**[48]

Jesus as role model

In the Gospel passage about Martha and Mary (Luke 10:38-42), we are on battle ground and Jesus sides with Mary. Why? Jesus recognises women's role is not in the kitchen! It is much more than dishing up meals and don't we just love Jesus for presenting women in such a positive light.

Jesus claims Mary 'has chosen the better part, which will not be taken away from her' (Luke 10:42). While Martha was 'distracted by her many tasks' we have Mary 'who sat at the Lord's feet and listened to what he was saying' (Luke 10:39). It is a positive attitude of attentive presence to the one before us, whom we hold in sacred space. We have today forgotten the special art of listening and genuine presence. Society must once again cultivate the practice of pastorally caring for another, in what has become a too fast paced world, that clamours in order to distract our attention from what really matters, the very people we are meant to spend close time with.

Like Martha, people today are so distracted by 'many tasks' that they have no time for relationships and what really matters. Mary indeed 'has chosen the better part,' that which is most needed towards another – time, patience, attentiveness, delight and love. All else is secondary.

---

[47]Annie Dillard, *Teaching a stone to talk*, (New York: Harper and Row, 1982), 20.
[48]Sheila Cassidy, *Light from the Dark Valley*, (London: Darton, Longman and Todd, 1994), 24.

Food can wait, cleaning can be done later. Now is the time to stop, to be present to the ones we love, to enjoy their company, to listen with love, before it's too late and they have walked out of our lives. As Joan Chittister writes:[49]

> Good friends have a way of being there - not daily, perhaps, but certainly when life demands their presence most. When their presence alone can bring meaning to the moment, they are always there.
>
> Only real friends can understand the depth of the pain and bring relief. They do not come as gawkers at a tragedy. They are at its center, bringing its balm, its comfort, its anodyne. It is understanding itself that divides the pain, makes grief possible. In front of my friend, there is no need to lie, to hold up like plastic on a stick, to press down the very emotion that is at this time the only proof of the life that's left in us.
>
> Finally, if the relationship is real, then fidelity itself will make possible the companionship that follows it through both darkness or light, pain or outrageous joy. Relationship takes loneliness away, makes abandonment impossible, promises life in the midst of death because the heart and the strength of the other enables us to face it.

What makes for a Pastoral carer

Deep within the hearts and minds of Christians is the invitation to embrace all of humanity with the tender love of Jesus. This is what is termed pastoral care. Yet how honest, willing or capable are we about approaching others and what quality of care do we provide? Such fears are the common lot of humankind:
- What am I meant to say?
- What if I make a mistake?
- What if they reject me?
- Will I know what to do?
- What help will I be?

---
[49] Joan Chittister, *Two Dogs and a Parrot: What Animals Can Teach Us About the Meaning of Life*, (New York: BlueBridge, 2015).

- I can't handle seeing someone in pain or suffering
- I'm too cold hearted to do this
- I haven't got the patience
- I don't have time
- I'm too emotional
- I'm not gentle enough
- I'm not good with words
- Others would be better at this than me

Whatever our excuses, others need our care and our care matters. If we are created in God's image, then we possess a heart that is moved with compassion, hands that can caress, ears that listen and a voice that can express what needs to be said.

So qualities in us that contribute towards caring for others include: a genuine love for others, trustworthiness, spiritual maturity, humility, genuineness, honesty, and the ability to channel God's grace. Other things the pastoral carer is called to do include:

- Be present
- Listen
- Gently enquire after people
- Empathise
- Generate hope
- Surround with love, patience and support
- Accept feelings no matter what they are or how unusual
- Maintain predictability and stability
- Use physical touch when appropriate
- Allow for silences for people to collect their thoughts
- Observe nonverbal messages
- Acknowledge what the loss means for the person
- Invite the person to talk about significant issues
- Invite the person to think about and take the next steps
- Encourage the person to seek further counsel if need be

- Confront or challenge the person
- Empower
- Advocate
- Ensure safety
- Seek justice
- Be a guide to seeking and understanding God's perspective
- Promote reconciliation – with God, Church, family, oneself
- Provide spiritual comfort and prayer
- Offer ongoing support to patient and family

As pastoral carers, it is vital to move people from a Drama Triangle where there are the victim, rescuer and persecutor, to a Winner's Triangle where the roles involve the vulnerable (instead of victim), the caring (instead of rescuer) and the assertive (instead of persecutor).[50]

Practical care

Although one may be hesitant to offer their presence and words, providing practical care often comes more naturally and is also important. Ways of offering practical care include:
- Provide a meal
- Send humorous, profound, or caring notes, letters and cards
- Phone
- Visit
- Invite them to something enjoyable such as a musical, car drive, footy game, coffee, etc.
- Bring gifts such as flowers
- Offer to read to them
- Repair broken things
- Bring in the mail
- Put out the garbage
- Baby sit

---

[50] Kate Litchfield, *Tend my flock. Sustaining good pastoral care*, (London: Canterbury Press, 2006), 74.

- Run errands
- Grocery shopping
- Gardening
- Ask how you can help

People grow and learn to cope with struggles, especially when supported emotionally and practically by others who show genuine care.

The do nots of pastoral care

As a pastoral carer, there are actions and words one should refrain from. Often we try to comfort with the following words[51]

- Don't worry
- It's all for the best
- You're tough, you can take it
- It's OK
- I know just how you feel
- It's God's will
- At least you have your faith
- It's not as bad as . . .
- They're better off now

Refrain from and don't:
- Try to rush the person out of their illness
- Suggest miracle cures
- Imply lack of prayer or faith
- Tell them what to feel or think
- Direct the conversation toward what seems important to you
- Interpret situations out of your own frame of reference
- Interrupt or finish their sentences
- Deny or argue with their version of reality
- Jump to conclusions

---

[51]Genevieve Glen, Marilyn Kofler and Kevin O'Connor, *Handbook for Ministers of Care* (Chicago: Liturgy Training Publications, 1997), 12.

- Insist the person talk about their issue
- Push for action
- Bypass the person's complaints and laments
- Question and instruct
- Reason and analyse
- Persuade and reassure
- Try to fix things
- Blame, criticise, shame or judge
- Give advice, moralise or preach
- Panic
- Name-calling
- Be angry or offended
- Save or rescue
- Fidget and watch the time

In other words, avoid playing the role of:
- Aggressor
- Distractor
- Peacemaker
- Clarifier
- Blocker
- Evaluator
- Information seeker
- Silent observer

Tesa Silvestre wrote down what her mother wanted to receive from those who came to offer care while she was terminally ill with cancer.[52]
- What do you find most helpful? Friends who ask me how I am doing rather than making assumptions. I like when people ask me: "How are you?" and "How do you feel?" That feels very different than people who say "I hope that you are feeling as good as you look" . . . I appreciate people who simply listen to what I have to

---

[52] Tesa Silvestre *My Mother's last Spring* A Network for Grateful Living on 12 July 2017 http://www.opw.catholic.org.au/latest-news/my-mother-s-last-spring.html?mc_cid=be645a6a95&mc_eid=33f1f9b328#.WXmEIYiGOUl

say, and don't volunteer advice without first asking me if I want it... It feels good when people are still able to be with me in sickness as they used to be when I was in good health: friendly, happy-going, calling me up, and inviting me to do things.

- And how about least helpful? People who respond through the lens of their own fear or discomfort and want me to feel better so that they can feel better. People who systematically avoid the topic of my illness and pretend that nothing is going on, or always want to talk about something else... People who try to fix me, rather than walk with me.

- What advice do you give to the friends and relatives of people with a severe illness? Let your loved one lead. Only talk about what they are actually ready to hear ... What people who are ill most need is to feel loved, to know that they matter... Another thing: gentle physical touch, like holding someone's hand, is very comforting to people who are afraid.

To offer pastoral care is not about us, what we say or do. Our role is to direct the person to God. Richard Rohr calls this the first and final work of all true religion. All else is secondary. Call it grace, enlightenment, peak experience, baptism in the Spirit, revelation, consciousness, growth, or surrender, but until such a threshold is passed, people are never helped in any true, lasting sense.[53] It's not about fixing or making it right. It's about touching the core of the person, their hearts, their deepest truth.

Emotions and values

> An old Cherokee Indian was talking to his grandson about a fight he felt within himself. In graphic images, the grandfather described a fight between two wolves. One of the wolves was evil and filled with regret, greed, self-pity, sorrow, pride, envy and anger. The other wolf was filled with generosity, truth, compassion, faith, humility, kindness, peace, love, joy and hope. The little grandson asked, 'Which wolf wins?' The old Cherokee said simply, 'The one I feed.'[54]

---

[53]Rohr, *What the mystics know. Seven pathways to your deeper self*, 138
[54]Native American Legends 'Two Wolves' A Cherokee Legend. http://www.firstpeople.us/FP-Html-Legends/TwoWolves-Cherokee.html

There is a major shift in Western culture, from the Christian ethic of duty, sacrifice and self-denial, towards a new ethic of the self, which says the most important goal in life, is the well-being of the self.[55] This has meant culture takes the interior, emotional life of the individual seriously and people make sense of the world through the prism of emotion.

Emotion comes from the Latin word *movere*, meaning to move. This movement involves the whole person. Emotions have a constructive role in the psychological, spiritual, religious and moral dimensions of human life.

Emotions can be a powerful source of energy and creativity, a source of healing when addressed well, toxic when not. We have control of our emotions. Desires and emotions are our capacity to know and appreciate true, objective values. They can be sacramental in quality, revelatory of the divine presence in our lives, and so attentiveness to them is required.

True values draw one out of oneself to self-transcendence. We see this especially in emotions such as courage, compassion, love and empathy. Or one moves away from what hinders achieving those values through fear, anger, guilt, shame and despair.

The danger with negative emotions is that in making one feel uncomfortable, one can think they are bad or morally wrong. Opening oneself to past agendas, distorted thoughts, hurtful ideas, and false beliefs, that lurk below the surface, can teach much. Carers need to provide others the space to allow these unexamined memories and perceptions to surface and to examine and address them with love and understanding.

However, barriers to sharing emotions include a sense of inferiority causing one to fear the response of the other, humiliating oneself, or one may not want to admit they need help. Yet even Jesus was open about his need for his disciples especially in the Garden of Gethsemane.

---

[55] Alan Billings, *Secular Lives, Sacred Hearts: The Role of the Church in a Time of No Religion*, (London: SPCK, 2004), 25.

One way to assist others to hear emotions is through the ANS Process:

Acknowledge	Name the emotion quietly to yourself; this will help you to take some distance from the emotion without disowning it.
Non-judgmental	Remind yourself that it is okay to feel this way. Emotions are friends, not enemies, bearing wisdom, not demons.
Stay with it	Listen to the emotion by asking open questions – don't answer the questions, just listen.

Presence

My brother's death led me to inner places I never dreamed I would go. One direction it aimed me was toward the constancy of divine presence. When my brother's death forced open the door, I stepped into grief and found the compassionate, all-embracing Holy One dwelling within me. I also discovered an inner resiliency I did not know I had, along with an ability to reach beyond self-pity toward a determined hope - **Joyce Rupp**[56]

Pastoral presence allows for true connection, and understanding deeply from the heart. It is in such presence that others experience the power of God that heals, sustains, reconciles and guides.

Time with another is referred to as 'holy ground' on which people become co-pilgrims on a spiritual journey. By being present, the carer has the intentionality to be open, to connect, and to honour mystery. When a carer is authentically present, permission is given for the other to become more present to their own life with its suffering, fear, hope, joy, etc. A pastoral presence committed to being good news, leads to growth and healing, as others come to know they are not alone. In their suffering and sorrow, as Richard Rohr says, the call is to meet people 'where they are at' and help them trust 'where they are not at.'[57]

---

[56]Joyce Rupp, *Open the door. A journey to the truth self,* (Notre Dame, Indiana: Sorin Books, 2008), 66-67.

[57]Rohr, *What the mystics know. Seven pathways to your deeper self,* 80.

Michael E. Cavanagh writes that the quality of being 'unconditionally' present to people means that whatever decisions people make and however far from the Kingdom their paths wander, the effective pastoral carer will always be at their side, attempting to shed light and bring assistance.[58]

For Elizabeth Lee, 'presence is more than compassionate listening; it is an opening up of myself to hear the vulnerability of the other in my being. It is a giving of myself such that I can be intensely attentive to the mystery of the other, aware that I am one with, in communion with, the other.'[59]

Compassion/Empathy/Mercy

The English word compassion comes from the Latin words *cum* and *pati* meaning *to suffer with*. It is about full immersion into the condition of being human through word, action and relationship. The Hebrew Scriptures uses the term *rachum*, meaning 'compassion' which comes from the word 'womb' and is the gut feeling of empathy with someone in need. Compassion/empathy is the ability to share in someone else's feelings, experiences, to understand their motivations, thoughts and fears almost as if they were our own. John Powell with Michael H. Cheney insightfully note:[60]

> We are all like mirrors to one another. We perceive ourselves largely in the 'feedback' of one another's reactions. We are always contributing, positively or negatively, to one another's self-image. I can know that I am worthwhile only in the mirror of your smiling face, only in the warm sound of your voice, and in the gentle touch of your hand. And you can understand your worth only in my face, my voice and my touch . . . the eyes of love see in every other person not one but two persons: the wounded and angry, the good and gifted. It is understanding and love that call forth the good and gifted person . . . Having given a listening and available heart in empathy, we must go

---
[58]Michael E Cavanagh, *The Effective Minister: Psychological and Social Considerations*, (San Francisco: Harper and Rowe, 1986), 30.
[59]Elizabeth Lee, 'Prison Ministry has Changed Me' in *Eremos* Sept 2014, no. 128. p. 18.
[60]John Powell with Michael H. Cheney, *A Life-Giving Vision: How to be a Christian in Today's world*, (Texas: Thomas More, 1995).

on to respond to the specific needs of those we love. The two specific needs we can be sure of are the gift of ourselves in self-disclosure and the gift of our affirmation of the other's worth.

Listening

What the other person has to say is important and deserves validation. So, listening is a decision to engage in another's life story and to discern how to be of help in the shaping of their story. Listening also requires an ability to hear what is being said with body language, with silence and in the words behind the words. Listening requires that we separate facts, feelings, and fiction.[61] So how do we listen?

- Attend - Look into the other person's eyes (depending on the culture). Position your body so they can see you. Focus on the other. Nod occasionally. Lean forward to express your interest and provide feedback. Stay attuned to the present and be in that moment. M. Scott Peck said that true listening requires a setting aside of oneself. Sensing this acceptance, the speaker will become more likely to open up the inner recesses of their mind to the listener.

- Invite self-disclosure - Stephen Covey said, 'Most of us don't listen with the intent to understand. We listen with the intent to reply'. Rather we should encourage the person to take all possible conversational initiative.[62] This is achieved by communicating acceptance and nonjudgmental care.

- Allow time for reflection.

- Attend to emotional communications - listen for clues to the person's inner life, such as hidden conflicts, unspoken desires, unspeakable fears, and faint hopes.

- Look around in addition to looking within - look carefully at and make evaluative judgments about the social environment that surrounds those who are the subjects of pastoral care.

---

[61]Willard W. C. and Ashley, Sr., 'Counseling and Interventions' in *Professional Spiritual & Pastoral Care: A Practical Clergy and Chaplains' Handbook*, edited by Stephen B. Roberts, (Nashville, TN: SkyLight Paths Publishing, 2013), 127.
[62]Celeste Headlee, TED Talks 10 ways to have a better conversation, Posted Feb 2016 http://www.ted.com/talks/celeste_headlee_10_ways_to_have_a_better_conversation/transcript?language=en

Even in situations in which a carer is recognised as having the primary responsibility for the care of another person, mutuality can be present and true listening means bringing myself, not just my care, to the encounter. It is in accepting the other as a whole person and being open enough to their experience and ideas that my own may change as a result of the interaction. By listening, one should be prepared to be amazed, to learn and to be transformed.

Communication

> The deepest level of communication is not communication, but communion. It is wordless. It is beyond words, and it is beyond speech, and it is beyond concept. - **Thomas Merton**[63]
> We say that we 'conduct' a conversation, but the more genuine a conversation is, the less its conduct lies within the will of either partner. Thus a genuine conversation is never the one that we wanted to conduct. Rather, it is generally more correct to say that we fall into conversation, or even that we become involved in it. The way one word follows another, with the conversation taking its own twists and reaching its own conclusion, may well be conducted in some way, but the partners conversing are far less the leaders of it than the led. No one knows in advance what will 'come out' of a conversation. Understanding or its failure is like an event that happens to us. Thus we can say that something was a good conversation or that it was ill fated. All this shows that a conversation has a spirit of its own, and that the language in which it is conducted bears its own truth within it – i.e. that it allows something to 'emerge' which henceforth exists.
> - **Hans-Georg Gadamer**[64]

Dialogue comes from two Greek roots, *dia*, meaning 'with each other,' and *logos*, meaning 'word' or 'speech,' suggesting the core meaning of shared speech. Dialogue is exploration and discovery through conversational engagement that increases awareness, understanding, and insight to self, others and the world.[65]

---

[63] Thomas Merton, Speech in Calcutta, 1968, *The Asian Journal of Thomas Merton*, p. 308.
[64] Hans-Georg Gadamer, *Truth and Method*, trans by Joel Weisheimer and Donald G Marshall, (Crossroad, 1989), 383.
[65] David G. Benner, *Care of Souls. Revisioning Christian Nurture and Counsel*, (Grand Rapids, Michigan: Baker Books, 1998), 131-132.

Conversation is derived from two Latin verbs:
- *Conversari*, meaning to dwell, 'keep company with' or 'abide'
- *Convertere*, meaning to change, convert, refresh or turn

This implies a twofold movement in conversation. The first, *conversari*, is a movement to face and be present to and for the other. The second, *convertere*, is a movement to face myself. Conversation is being prepared to face the other, in respect, openness and courtesy, with the expectation that oneself and the other are in search for truth and goodness. So, ways to better communicate include:

1. Repeat – when you repeat, the other will continue with their line of thought. Repeating will help you listen. Repetition honours the speaker's choice of words and offers them back as a way for continued dialogue. Literal interpretation also helps the speaker hear what has just been said and so stimulates further reflection on the words chosen.[66]

2. Restate/paraphrase - takes small chunks of dialogue and rewords them sensitively. The goal is to let the other hear their words from another vantage point and process them further. This allows the other to go more deeply in their thoughts, to explore and gain further insight.

3. Reflect – the carer acts as a mirror for the emotional content of the other's words. A listener who can accurately identify the speaker's emotion communicates that the conveyed emotional content has been received and deemed important enough for attention.[67]

4. Respond – entails absorbing what the speaker says and then offering it back in order to bring the dialogue to a deeper level. It involves attending to the entirety of the speaker's message, hearing the speaker's words, and discerning the emotions behind them.

Pastoral carers help one to explore the inner world of the other, through open and relevant questions, allowing time for reflective response through silence and supportive verbal and nonverbal

---

[66]Robert A. Kidd, 'Foundational listening and responding skills' in *Professional Spiritual & Pastoral Care: A Practical Clergy and Chaplain's Handbook*, edited by Stephen B. Roberts, (SkyLight Paths Publishing, US, 2013), 94.

[67]Kidd, 'Foundational listening and responding skills' in *Professional Spiritual & Pastoral Care: A Practical Clergy and Chaplain's Handbook*, 95.

affirmations. Well placed, open-ended questions at the beginning of a conversation invite care seekers to tell their stories. Questions with who, what, when, where, why or how, makes them stop and think. However, a bombardment of questions usually puts the caregiver in charge of the conversation, especially at the outset, and indicates the caregiver's need to know information.[68]

Hovering is beneficial when a topic is painful, risky or overwhelming to the speaker while buffering responses helps soften the impact of difficult or hard-to-express emotions or topics and clear the way for more vulnerable interchanges.

- You may not want to talk about this now, but . . .
- I'm sorry you've been feeling so awful. I'm glad you're still here
- I'm here for you. Remember that you can always talk to me if you need to
- I want to help you. Tell me what I can do to support you

Silence allows for a deeper sense of understanding. There is also nonverbal communication which includes:
- facial expression
- eye contact
- smile
- tears
- laughter
- body posture
- nodding
- dress/clothing
- touch/contact
- closeness/distance
- tone of voice

As Saint Camillus states, 'Put more heart into your hands.' In communication, one needs to set aside all desires except love and focus on the facts of soul and spirit. The pastoral carer invites moral reflection and offers judicious advice, suggestions or direction.

---

[68]Carrie Doehring, *The Practice of Pastoral Care: A Postmodern Approach* (Kentucky: Westminster John Knox Press, 2015), 63.

Tesa Silvestre was asked by her terminally ill mother, "Do you think I'll make it?" I spoke what was true: "I really hope you will, but I really don't know what is going to happen." . . . Later, when my mother was in the final days of her life at the hospital, I got to talk with a colleague of hers who used to work in her palliative care unit. When, I told him about our exchange, he said sweetly: The best way to let them lead is to answer their question with a question. "Why are you asking? Are you feeling anxious and needing to be reassured?"[69]

Prayer

Prayer can be a time when God provides that nurturing, healing touch which frees and empowers not only the person in need of care, but also the giver of care. Jesus took time out to pray (Mark 1:35) and the disciples desired to pray too (Luke 11:1).

Prayer should be used to affirm the presence of God and to inspire hope in patients who are worried, anxious, or feeling guilty, and for families who are grieving.

There are two forms of praying: ritual prayer (from tradition) and prayer-as-listening. Both are responses in faith to circumstances and belief about oneself and belief about God.

Prayers from ritual/tradition include the Lord's Prayer, Hail Mary, Psalms, hymns, rosary, litanies, rite of communion for the sick and dying. These prayer forms can be valuable resources in care, but also a defence against intimacy due to emotional isolation and repetition.

Prayer-as-listening is of the moment, existential and dialogical. This is the prayer of listening to the Spirit, recognising God's movement in our lives. The ability to grasp what is essentially at the heart of a patient's concern is the first step towards expressing deep prayer.

The person seeking care may resist becoming aware of and transforming their experience through prayer because it involves struggle, negotiating danger, coping with pain, trying to achieve some sort of security, questions are asked, and experiences are remembered. But through conversation and gentle presence, reassurance can take

---

[69]Tesa Silvestre *My Mother's last Spring* A Network for Grateful Living on 12 July 2017 http://www.opw.catholic.org.au/latest-news/my-mother-s-last-spring.html?mc_cid=be645a6a95&mc_eid=33f1f9b328#.WXmEIYiGOUl

place, answers can arise, and hope embraced. So praying with others is important because it:
- Activates the faith process
- Provides words to their needs
- Allows them to share their concerns with God
- Gives them an openness to God
- Acknowledges that God is in control
- Offers an acceptance of life's challenges
- Equips one with courage to face problems
- Can bring comfort
- Alleviates anxiety
- Sustains one through the crisis
- Can bring a change of heart
- Offers physical healing
- Heals broken relationships
- Offers reconciliation with a loved one
- Remains a universal answer

Since praying with another can trigger very deep emotions and can be a profound spiritual experience, care needs to be taken never to misuse it to manipulate or coerce the individual towards the pastoral carer's point of view.

Reflection

They don't tell us it is important.
For if the truth were to be told,
the power to care
Would unleash uncontrollable capacity in others.
There is an aura about such people who know how to truly care
They make you feel so at ease
You want to open up
To be better.
They make life seem abundantly good.
How we desire to be like those people.
Just by their positive power
Their calming tone
Their words of encouragement
Their perceptive insights
The warmth of their touch
The depth in their eyes
Their gentle presence
Their wise ways
Their assuring look
Their compassionate nature
Their ability to discern
Their care that matters
Their love that is boundless.
They carry the true human spirit
They make us better people
They are the unsung heroes. Amen.

Chapter 6:
Ethical dimension and self-care

> Lord, make me an instrument of your peace; where there is hatred, let me sow love; where there is injury, pardon; where there is doubt, faith; where there is despair, hope; where there is darkness, light; and where there is sadness, joy. O Divine Master, grant that I may not so much seek to be consoled as to console; to be understood, as to understand; to be loved, as to love; for it is in giving that we receive, it is in pardoning that we are pardoned, and it is in dying that we are born to Eternal Life. - **Saint Francis of Assisi**

Code of Ethics

Pastoral care involves a commitment of time, energy, ongoing training and accountability. Given the professional character of the ministry, it necessitates a code of ethics to foster authentic ministry.

A code of ethics aims to assure the public of the trustworthiness of those called to pastoral care. A code also provides a set of standards that define, interpret and measure responsible pastoral practice. It makes explicit the primary values that should govern personal growth in professional identity and basic moral obligations that mark professional responsibilities in the exercise of ministry.[70]

However a Code of Ethics has limitations. First, it does not guarantee compliance. Secondly, a code does not prevent lawsuits. Thirdly, a limitation of a code is its proper interpretation.

What is power?

The ability to influence another person's behaviours, thoughts, emotions or attitudes is termed power. It is derived from a variety of sources including:

---

[70] Richard M. Gula, *Just Ministry. Professional Ethics for Pastoral Ministers*, (New York: Paulist Press, 2010), 39.

- Money
- Possessions
- Physical health
- Strength
- Age
- Gender
- Colour
- Ethnic origin
- Educational attainment
- Social status
- Size
- Physical attractiveness
- Experience
- Reputation
- Emotional stability
- Charisma
- Language skills
- Personality
- Knowledge
- Competence

These personal sources of power are at work in pastoral relationships and so carers need to be careful they are not influencing or manipulating situations of encounters.

Kate Litchfield notes that, typically, boys and men are encouraged to develop confidence in exercising power. The energy and vitality which this power brings can be used in creative initiatives. However, with emphasis on men feeling they have to be strong and the consequent pressure on them to deny feelings, there arises issues of vulnerability and weakness that need to be addressed by a pastoral carer.[71]

---

[71] Kate Litchfield, *Tend my flock. Sustaining good pastoral care*, (London: Canterbury Press, 2006), 43.

Girls and women are more likely to be socialised to be passive and responsive rather than to initiate, a pattern reinforced by the way their bodies surrender to the processes of life. The positive side of this can be a willingness to wait and trust, to be attentive, enabling things to happen rather than forcing the pace. Yet women may need to be aware of a tendency to manipulate in situations where they feel powerless. Pastoral carers are invited to encourage women to exercise their power and authority in ways that are transparent and unambiguous.[72]

Official appointment as a pastoral minister or Ordination also confers a particular authority/power which can be extremely influential upon lay people. Such authority encompasses institutional authority of official appointment, and the authority from God to be a symbolic representative of the community of faith. There is a 'sacred weight' that adds more seriousness to what they say and do.

Ordained ministers who are insecure, or feel that their authority is threatened, may compensate by misusing authority to bolster their fragile self-esteem or enhance their status and power in relation to lay people, rather than seeing it as something to be used to empower the faith community. Or they may use religious power and authority and the concept of Christian obedience to coerce others into certain behaviours or beliefs which they would not ordinarily freely choose.[73]

Transference/Projection

The inequality of power on pastoral relationships may evoke feelings in the person being helped that derive from childhood relationships with authority figures and carers, particularly mothers, fathers and teachers. When this happens, the person may feel helpless, childlike and vulnerable. This is referred to as transference/projection when the person 'transfers' their feelings, expectations and behaviours from previous relationships to the pastoral carer. Likewise, countertransference occurs when the pastoral carer may experience feelings towards the person they are helping, which derive from their own past relationships.[74]

---
[72] ibid, 45.
[73] ibid, 38, 50.
[74] ibid, 47.

Transfer/Projection is a process of letting people's unconscious hopes, fears and defences become conscious. Pastoral carers require maturity in handling situations where people project their anger, fear, guilt and need onto them. With sensitivity, pastoral carers can use the projections to help people clarify their thoughts and feelings about their relationship to God and others.[75]

Boundaries

Boundaries are an essential safeguard in relationship with other people, enabling pastoral carers to respect and protect their own and other people's autonomy and space. Some of the boundaries that carers must establish and maintain are those of time, space and person.

Boundaries of time give security, safety and respect the other. It is good practice for the carer to suggest how long the meeting might be for and to check whether this is a convenient length of time for the other person. Working within a time-frame of twenty-five to fifty minutes is best practice, but one must keep in mind some cultures are more flexible about starting and stopping meetings at a set time. Failure to maintain clear time boundaries can result in both parties feeling unsafe.

Boundaries of space include where to meet in order to protect confidentiality and to safeguard against any risk of misunderstanding, abuse, exploitation or false accusation. Changing the setting or the environment can confuse, threaten or distract the one seeking the pastoral service.[76] Where a carer is concerned about a meeting, they should establish safeguards including notifying a colleague of the scheduled meeting, time and place. It is important to make it clear to the other person that others are aware of the meeting. A carer must also consider whether to meet people in their homes, how the chairs are arranged, sitting position, if the door should be opened or closed, and whether there is anyone else on the premises.

The act of entrusting comes from the one seeking the ministerial service so professional ministerial relationships are not mutually

---

[75]Richard M. Gula, *Just Ministry. Professional Ethics for Pastoral Ministers*, (New York: Paulist Press, 2010), 128.
[76]ibid, 130

reciprocal. The pastoral carer does not entrust matters of personal concern to others and so is less vulnerable and at less risk. However, when ministers disclose personal information about themselves, they need to reflect carefully on their motivation for doing so. There are occasions were self-disclosure by the pastoral carer can establish a greater degree of equality in a pastoral relationship. However, there is also a risk that self-disclosure will be used to manipulate a response from the other person.[77] In considering boundaries, warning signs of over-involvement include:
- Becoming preoccupied with thoughts and fantasies about a person
- Dreaming or lying awake at night thinking about them
- Finding excuses for seeing the person
- Failing to tell others about meetings with the person
- Exchanging personal or significant gifts and concealing this from others
- Taking particular care of appearance when meeting the person
- Seeking or allowing unnecessary or lingering physical contact
- Avoiding the person or experiencing anxiety and embarrassment about meeting them
- Underlying fear of attraction
- Sense that there is an element of risk in the relationship
- Can't say no to the person
- Over-reacting to statements that the person makes
- Inability to end the relationship and let another carer take over

The Catholic Church in Australia's publication *Integrity in Ministry* notes that there must be respect for 'the physical and emotional boundaries appropriate to relationships with adults and minors.' Among the behavioural standards that follow from this principle are:
- exercising sensitivity with regard to the physical and emotional space others require in pastoral encounters
- exercising a prudent judgment that has the well-being of the other as its goal, in initiating and responding to physical contact, such as giving a comforting hug or an affirming touch

---

[77] Litchfield, *Tend my flock. Sustaining good pastoral care*, 90.

- providing pastoral ministry only in places that offer a sufficiently safe environment where there is openness and visibility
- exercising prudent judgment in the expression of affection and regard, and in the giving of gifts.[78]

Sexual violation

The informality of pastoral ministry can give freedom to hug and extend other friendly gestures of touch, in a way that would not be open to any other profession. Sensitive touch can offer deep comfort and communicate compassionate understanding. However, people at times of crisis are also extremely vulnerable and require great sensitivity and care.[79] In relationships of unequal power, it is unusual for the less powerful person to initiate touch and the other person's freedom to refuse any form of touch must be respected.

Sexual abuse in ministry is about the betrayal of trust and the misuse of power. It occurs when a minister misuses their pastoral position for personal sexual gain. In recent years, media attention has ensured that it is an issue addressed in response to both the perpetrators and victims of abuse. There are two principles operative in discussing boundary violations of a sexual nature:

1. The professional always has more responsibility than anyone else. The burden is on pastoral persons to maintain a professional relationship with the patient or family.
2. Sexual activity between the minister and person in need of care is always harmful to the unsuspecting individual. The principle is based on the power differential between the professional and the recipient of care. To consent to sexual activity is usually never free or mutual, because the recipient is influenced by transference.[80]

Pastoral care persons need to be aware of their sexuality. They are constantly relating to people, not through their role, but as human beings who have a sexual dimension. It is important for them to have

---

[78]*Integrity in Ministry. A Document of Principles and Standards for Catholic Clergy & Religious in Australia.* Reprinted 2010. Paragraph 1.4 https://www.catholic.org.au/documents/1344-integrity-in-ministry-2010-1/file

[79]Litchfield, *Tend my flock. Sustaining good pastoral care*, 83.

[80]Gerald R. Niklas, *The Making of a Pastoral Person*, (New York: Alba House, 2001), 121.

close friends and a strong support system so they can have their needs for intimacy met in these relationships, rather than taking advantage of those who come for care and help.[81]

The 'Truth, Justice and Healing Council' was established to assist those who were sexually abused by the Catholic Church in Australia. It's opening lines state:[82]

> Towards Healing offers a person who has been abused, by a priest or religious or other Church personnel, the opportunity to tell his or her story, personally and directly, to someone in authority in the Church, who will accept responsibility for what happened to him or her, acknowledge the damage he or she has suffered, give a sincere apology, and offer pastoral care and reparation.

Dual Roles

When one interacts with another person in more than one role, dual relationships occur, bringing the possibility of confusion about the role and the risk of transgressing boundaries. Often, dual relationships can be managed when things are going well, but when problems arise in one role which impacts on another role, they become difficult to sustain. There is also the risk that the pastoral carer's own interests will cloud their ability to judge what is appropriate ethical behaviour.[83]

Dual relationships require the pastoral minister to be self-aware, to focus on keeping the pastoral role as the primary relationship, and to pay attention to any potential for role conflict or 'leakage' between the different roles. To keep the relationship clear, Richard M. Gula, suggests asking these question:[84]

- Which role is dominant for me in this relationship?
- Who am I for you in this relationship?
- Who are you for me?
- Whose needs are being met here?

---

[81]Gerald R. Niklas, *The Making of a Pastoral Person*, (New York: Alba House, 2001), 122.

[82]*Truth, Justice and Healing Council*. Royal Commission into Institutional Responses to Child Sexual Abuse Issues. Paper No. 2 Towards Healing, 30 September 2013, Paragraph 1.1 http://www.tjh-council.org.au/media/39435/30549468_2_TJHC-Towards-Healing-submission-30-Sep-2013.pdf

[83]Litchfield, *Tend my flock. Sustaining good pastoral care*, 82.

[84]Gula, *Just Ministry. Professional Ethics for Pastoral Ministers*, 137.

Reflecting as a pastoral carer

Plato says, 'the unreflected life is not worth living'. This integrated awareness of inner and outer reality, this sense of self, is linked with growth in one's humanity and wisdom. Engaging one's faith in the reflective process occurs in two ways:

- Reflection–in-action: occurs while we are involved with a task and we are making meaning as we go. Questions include: What is going on here? What do I need to do?
- Reflection-on-action: occurs intentionally after the activity has stopped. Questions include: What happened? How did I respond? What did I do well? What worried me about the situation? What could I have done better or differently?

Discernment in complex pastoral situations requires the discipline of prayer, silence, sacrament, Bible study, reflection, rest and a willingness to listen and learn by example. Sally and Paul Nash offer guidelines to test the outcome of one's actions:[85]

- Is it in harmony with our understanding of the Bible?
- Is it coherent with our values?
- Does it build the kingdom of God?
- Do I have an inner peace?
- Do I sense the Holy Spirit?
- Will it bring life?
- Can I do this with integrity?
- Is it in line with my personal and/or professional ethics?
- Have I discussed this with others in my community? Why? Why not?

To be theologically reflective, one needs to watch, look, listen, ask questions, have an ability to judge, discern, apply wisdom and identify the consequences of one's actions.

---

[85]Sally Nash and Paul Nash, *Tools for reflective ministry*, (London: SPCK, 2009), 6.

Burnout

Those involved in the helping professions, such as pastoral care, are particularly vulnerable to burnout. Difficulties a person faces which can contribute to burnout include:

- The job of pastoral care is never finished
- Pastoral care is difficult to measure and assess
- One is dealing constantly with people's expectations of them
- Involves a variety of tasks to be performed alongside expected personal qualities of goodness
- Takes energy to contend with the rejection, criticism and hostility of people
- The pastoral carer must deal with the same people year after year
- Dealing with many people who are in search of a person to cling to, to be made to feel important, to hide from life's difficulties, or to find a situation they can dominate, is difficult and draining to the carer
- People are not comfortable with God in their lives. They prefer to talk to a pastoral carer and so can be evasive of the truth they need to address

One cannot care for others and not become emotionally involved. Yet, on the other hand, if one becomes too emotionally involved, one will not be an effective carer. All too often pastoral carers, instead of practising prayer, which brings people into the presence of God, enter into the practice of Messiah: they do the work of God for God, fix people up, tell them what to do, conspire in finding shortcuts by which the long journey to the Cross can be bypassed.[86]

As a result of the demands on a pastoral carer, they may experience burnout. Each person has signals or symptoms that their bodies alert them to when they are under too much stress including:

- Tired
- Anxious
- Panic attacks

---

[86] Eugene H. Peterson, *The Contemplative Pastor. Returning to the Art of Spiritual Direction*, (Grand Rapids, Michigan: William B. Eerdmans Publishing Company, 1989), 43.

- Shortness of breath
- Headaches
- Nausea
- Cold/flu symptoms
- Sleep disruption
- Short tempered or irritable
- Abusive
- Cynical
- Cranky

It is important to understand how one reacts to stress and how to manage it. Self-care is essential. Aside from offering care to others, one must care for themselves too.

Self-care

It is important to give oneself permission to pull back from time to time. Jesus set an example in Luke 9:10, 'On their return the apostles told Jesus all they had done. He took them with him and withdrew privately to a city called Bethsaida.' Being clear about one's capacity and commitments actually helps others in the long run. Spiritually, it is essential to have space:[87]

- Before you begin each day, so that you are centred before beginning to see others
- Between seeing people so that you don't contaminate people with the issues of the last one
- Once your day is done, so you don't contaminate your family at home or remain absorbed with the negativity you may have experienced during the day

Having such spaces of time is a necessity. Otherwise, the depletion of energy and the destruction of a healthy perspective will start to take place. So, in healthy self-care, a number of suggestions include:

- Handover the situations to God in prayer
- Recognise that love is ever present

---

[87]Robert J. Wicks, *The Inner Life of the Counselor* (New Jersey: John Wiley & Sons, 2012), 5-6.

- Develop a circle of friends who will challenge, support, nurture and inspire
- Relax during the week
- Exercise regularly
- Set healthy boundaries on your energies as you have limited resources
- Take time for yourself, by saying to people, 'I am not able to help you now'
- Take time to do what gives you pleasure e.g. cooking, hobbies
- Write or journal
- Listen to music
- Go for walks
- Be aware of your own needs and wants
- Give yourself priority when appropriate

Reflection

Moments of joy arise when we care for another
When we flash a smile
Or lend a helping hand
Or are confided in by someone who trusts us.
Yet sometimes the grievances shared with us can be burdening.
We hear of sad stories, we know of bad experiences,
We are asked to help those in desperate need.
And we want to.
But sometimes we aren't the best person we can be
And we feel we have nothing to give
Or we don't know what else to do
Or we have become too exhausted
With repetitive demands and issues that never seem to heal.
But as you said, Jesus,
'Listen, I am casting out demons and performing cures
today and tomorrow,
and on the third day I finish my work' (Luke 13:32).
So we turn to you, God, time and time again,
For our nurture, for grace, for your Holy Spirit,
So that we can be love to others, wherever, whenever, and always.
Amen.

Chapter 7: Meaning of suffering

By the sweat of your face you shall eat bread until you return to the ground, for out of it you were taken; you are dust, and to dust you shall return. - **Genesis 3:19**
Give sorrow words. The grief that does not speak
Whispers the o'erfraught heart and bids it break.
- **Macbeth**[88]
Those who have known pain profoundly are the ones most wary of uttering the clichés about suffering. Experience with the mystery takes one beyond the realm of ideas and produces finally a muteness or at least a reticence to express in words the solace that can only be expressed by an attitude of union with the sufferer - **John Howard Griffin**[89]

Suffering can be manifested as physical, social, emotional and spiritual, and can trigger existential questions such as:
Why am I suffering?
Why am I here?
What is the meaning of my life?
What happens when I die?
Is there a benevolent God?
Will I be forgiven?
Why is this happening?

They are not easy questions to answer. Sooner or later one will deal with the issue of suffering which is part of human life, though felt more acutely in times of injustice, illness, ageing or nearing death. Pastoral care is the call to be involved with the grief, suffering and pain of others.

---

[88]William Shakespeare, *Macbeth* Act 4, Scene 3
[89]John Howard Griffin, *Prison of Culture: Beyond Black Like Me*, (Texas: Wings Press, 2011), 109.

Suffering as gleaned from the Scriptures

In the Scriptures, we come across numerous accounts of suffering. In the story of Jacob's wrestle with God (Genesis 32:23-32), he is left limping after the encounter. Yet in his struggle there emerges out of the fear, vulnerability and scarring, a new faith, courage, self-acceptance, compassion and a new sense of purpose to life. As Joan Chittister notes, the insights into meaning come through the experience of wrestling with God. Struggle transforms. It gives life depth, insight and compassion. When we know the meaning of what it is to struggle with something in life that stretches the spirit, we are worthy to walk with others in struggle, ready to listen and able to lead.[90]

In 1 Kings 19, the Prophet Elijah finds himself facing imminent persecution and death, and fear and depression accompany him. Why go on when there appears to be no reward in the struggle of life? Elijah calls out, 'I alone am left.' It is the universal human cry of injustice and loneliness. Does life have any real meaning or is it best that the Lord, 'take it away' (1 Kings 19:10).

In his struggle, Elijah stands on Mt Horeb, alone, searching, wanting a response that will assure him all will be well. Turmoil tosses him about as his world view seems to collapse before his eyes. Earthquake, fire and fury devour, and Elijah is storm tossed. Where is God? Why should life be like this?

Only when Elijah can let go of the questions and seek God can the confusion subsist and peace reign with 'a sound of sheer silence' (1 Kings 19:12). God alone redeems the protests, doubts and exhaustion of believers.

In the Book of Job, the dilemma concerns the collapse of his world of meaning. Job's friends were persuaded that by sin, Job had brought his sufferings upon himself and his troubles were evidence that God had cast him off. Job, convinced that his suffering was innocent, questioned this isolation but in his misfortune, Job neither compromises his dignity nor admits to something false. He probes for a resolution, governed by the principle that God must be powerful and just, and that Job is undeserving of such affliction.

---

[90]Joan Chittister, *Scarred by Struggle. Transformed by hope. The Process of Struggle*, (Grand Rapids, Michigan: William B Eerdmans Pub. Co. 2003), 83.

God neither reveals to Job why he is suffering, nor enters into the debate about the problem of evil (Chapters 38 to 41). Job must realise that the mystery of suffering is beyond solving. The profoundest answer to undeserved suffering resides in divine-human encounter. The relationship with God is more important than answers to our 'why?' Job had seen a vision of God who is victorious over all, entering into a larger freedom and proper perspective of his place in the universe, realising the human situation can be safely left to God (42:2). It is in compassionate relationship that the one who suffers discovers redemption.

The Book of Lamentations expresses the grief of a people who have known war, exile, alienation, suffering and loss. A lament is a particular form of prayer, that takes the brokenness of human experience to God for an answer. Stunned, sad and silenced by the tragedy and absurdity of human events, lament is an honest form of prayer that expresses rage, anger, hurt and disappointment. Yet lament's endpoint is reconciliation with and a deeper love of God, bounded by trust and hope that God is active in the world.

Believers who suffer may have strong convictions that the faithful response to suffering is passive acceptance. It will be important that carers help facilitate the possible dormant feelings of rage, frustration and doubt, to encourage them to lament and question, rather than resign to fate.

Jesus' suffering

In Jesus we witness to a divine love that passes through human toil, anguish and death. In the Garden of Gethsemane (Mark 14:32-42), Jesus is fully aware that suffering is close at hand. The pressing thought weighs down on him and he heads to a quiet space to pray, gather his thoughts and meet God.

The disciples gather too. In the presence of Peter, James and John, he 'began to be distressed and agitated' (Mark 14:33). Jesus needs reassurance, the comforting presence of friends, even though there may be no comforting words to voice, 'I am deeply grieved, even to death; remain here and keep awake' (Mark 14:34). A person in deep distress is in danger of falling into despair.

Jesus' journey to Golgotha and his crucifixion are laden with great suffering and torment. On the cross, Jesus cries, 'Eloi, Eloi, lema sabachthani?' which means, 'My God, my God, why have you forsaken me?' (Mark 15:34). This cry is heard from sufferers who experience forsakenness from others and from God.

The self-emptying love, even to death, reveals the shape of God's love because it enters into our weakness and feels our pain. Death on the cross means to suffer and die as one rejected, humiliated and cast out. The connection between the ministry of Jesus and his death on the cross is the ultimate expression of Jesus' commitment to give life to others. As Dietrich Bonhoeffer notes with deep insight:

> In the face of death we cannot simply speak in some fatalistic way, 'God wills it'; but we must juxtapose it with the other reality, 'God does not will it.' Death reveals that the world is not as it should be but that it stands in need of redemption. Christ alone is the conquering of death. Here the sharp antithesis between 'God wills it' and 'God does not will it' comes to a head and also finds its resolution. God accedes to that which God does not will, and from now on death itself must therefore serve God. From now on, the 'God wills it' encompasses even the 'God does not will it.' God wills the conquering of death through the death of Jesus Christ. Only in the cross and resurrection of Jesus Christ has death been drawn into God's powers, and it must now serve God's own aims. It is not some fatalistic surrender but rather a living faith in Jesus Christ, who died and rose for us, that is able to cope profoundly with death. In life with Jesus Christ, death as a general fate approaching us from without is confronted by death from within, one's own death, the free death of daily dying with Jesus Christ. Those who live with Christ die daily to their own will. Christ in us gives us over to death so that he can live within us. Thus our inner dying grows to meet that death from without. Christians receive their own death in this way, and in this way our physical death very truly becomes not the end but rather the fulfilment of our life with Jesus Christ. Here we enter into community with the One who at his own death was able to say, 'It is finished.'[91]

---

[91] Eric Metaxas, *Bonhoeffer. Pastor, Martyr, Prophet, Spy. A righteous gentile vs. the third reich*, (Nashville: Thomas Nelson, 2010), 384.

Sacrifice comes from the words *sacrum facere* - to make sacred or holy. A sacrifice does not mean that God is pleased by pain. Rather, it is an offering of the self for the other. When we go beyond the call of duty, when we lay our life down for others, those for whom we make such a sacrifice are able to believe our love and believe that they can do the same. Thus, redemptive suffering always generates immense life in others.[92] The struggles of the cross can transform the human spirit and leads to the emergence of new attitudes, motivations, sensitivity and forgiving love. This is what salvation is. Salvation from *salus*, means healing.

Through his holocaust experience, Elie Wiesel wrote his famous 'Night.' His interpretation is that God is dead on the gallows. There can be no God if there is such inhumanity:

> One day, when we came back from work, we saw three gallows rearing up in the assembly place, three black crows. Roll call. SS all around us; machine guns trained; the traditional ceremony. Three victims in chains - and one of them sad-eyed angel. The SS seemed more preoccupied than usual. To hang a young body in front of thousands of spectators was no light matter. The head of the camp read the verdict. All eyes were on the child. He was lividly pale, almost calm, biting his lip. The gallows threw shadows over him. This time the Lagerkapo refused to act as executioner. Three SS replaced him. The three necks were placed at the same moment within the nooses.
>
> 'Long live liberty!' cried the two adults. But the child was silent.
> 'Where is God? Where is He?' someone behind me asked.
> At a sign from the head of the camp, the three chairs tipped over. Total silence throughout the camp. On the horizon, the sun was setting.
> 'Bare your heads!' yelled the head of the camp. His voice was raucous. We were weeping.
> 'Cover your heads!'
> Then the march past began. The two adults were no longer alive. Their tongues hung swollen, blue-tinged. But the third

---

[92]Richard Rohr, *What the mystics know. Seven pathways to your deeper self*, (New York: The Crossroad Publishing company, 2015), 126.

rope was still moving; being so light, the child was still alive. For more than half an hour he stayed there, struggling between life and death, dying in slow agony before our eyes. And we had to look him full in the face. He was still alive when I passed in front of him. His tongue was still red, his eyes were not yet glazed. Behind me, I heard the same man asking, 'Where is God now?'

And I heard a voice within me answer him; 'Where is he? Here he is - he is hanging there on the gallows.' [93]

Elie's 'Night' can also be understood as a claim that God is another Jew that is killed, like so many Jews before and after him. However, from a Christian perspective, we would understand 'Night' as revealing God there on the gallows, suffering with us, but assured God will also redeem us.

Reasons for suffering

In the ancient world, suffering was viewed in varying ways including it was human fate to suffer, or that the gods had been offended and so they punished humans. Plagues, wars, natural disasters such as the ancient Babylonian flood story, were attempts by the gods to silence humans. The Greek gods were viewed as playing with humans for their amusement. Others believed suffering was the result of the gods of order clashing with the gods of chaos, such as Leviathan and Behemoth. A later version of this 'eternal combat' theory was that there was a good god and a bad god constantly battling each other. The Persian form of this belief was called Zoroastrianism. The Stoics taught that the goal in life was to reject the material in order to become more spiritual and that suffering was the way to learn patience.[94]

A reason for God allowing suffering has generally been supposed to consist of a benefit to some group or to the sufferer, that could not be gained without suffering. Other explanations given over time for suffering include:

---

[93] Elie Wiesel, *Night*, (New York: Bantam Books, 1982), 35.
[94] Jude Winkler, *I cry to you, O Lord! Scriptural reflections on the mystery and meaning of suffering*, (Maryland: The Word among us Press, 2008), 19-20.

- A means of expiation, purification or sanctification
- An expression of human imperfection
- A school of life
- An absurdity
- A mystery to accept
- A call to conversion
- Predestination or fatalism
- Outside forces or superstition

Geoffrey Robinson lists reasons that religious communities have come up with in order to explain suffering:[95]

1. Suffering is a punishment for sin – an ancient conviction but it does not fit the facts as many bad people prosper and many good people suffer.
2. Evil may prosper for a time but in the long run right will triumph – wishful thinking, an attempt to defend God rather than speak directly to the victims of evil and suffering.
3. God has good reasons for all that happens. We see only the loose threads at the back but God sees the beautiful tapestry on the other side – God would be using people without their consent and often against their will.
4. Parents must often make their children do things they do not want to do. It is for their good. God does the same to us through suffering – Parents never inflict pain solely so that children will learn to bear pain. If we accept suffering comes from God as a lesson to us, the next logical step would be a resigned fatalism.
5. Suffering is sent as a test to strengthen us and God will never ask more of us than we can bear – but many people fail the test and are overwhelmed by their suffering. For even the most fervent believers, there are moments when, in the face of suffering, belief appears useless and the 'comforts' of religion meaningless.
6. Death releases us from the pain of this world – hardly an answer to parents of a baby who has died. It is an attempt to do away with bad by calling it good.

---

[95]Geoffrey Robinson, *Travels in Sacred Places*, (Victoria: Harper Collins Religious, 1997), 186.

With assistance and grace, one can reach spiritual adulthood under physical, moral, social, and spiritual pressures, if one stays with painful tensions and sufferings long enough, as one does in the dark night of the soul, until they birth compassion, forgiveness and love. Viktor E. Frankl wrote that everything can be taken from a person but one thing: the last of the human freedoms - to choose one's attitude in any given set of circumstances.

> We had to teach the despairing men that *it did not really matter what we expected from life, but rather what life expected from us* . . . Life ultimately means taking the responsibility to find the right answer to its problems and to fulfil the tasks which it constantly sets for each individual . . .
>
> A man who becomes conscious of the responsibility he bears toward a human being who affectionately waits for him, or to an unfinished work, will never be able to throw away his life. He knows the 'why' for his existence, and will be able to bear almost any 'how' . . .[96]

Ways a pastoral carer can be there for those undergoing torment and suffering include:

- Allow them to express highly charged outrage geared at you or God
- Their demand to be heard must be honoured
- Listen and respond to the demure 'please help me'
- Give them permission to give voice to strong issues
- Help to release their tethered soul by being present without judging or condemning
- Draw them slowly out of the bitterness by your gentle patience
- Move them away from perpetually blaming God
- Help redirect one's energy toward eventual reconciliation and acceptance
- Journey with them until they arrive at a place of resolution

Meaning in suffering is not found in the cause, but in the result. The important question is, 'How are you going to respond to the suffering that has entered your life?' Even if specific answers are not found, one

---

[96]Victor Frankl, *Man's search for meaning*, (Boston: Beacon Press, 2006), 77, 80.

can come to an acceptance of not having the answer and being with the unknown. As Jude Winkler writes, 'God doesn't always make it all better, but God does make all the difference. If I know in the deepest part of my heart that God is there for me and that God will always be there for me no matter what happens, then I can trust. I can find the strength to say, "Not my will, but your will be done."'[97]

---

[97] Jude Winkler, *I cry to you, O Lord! Scriptural reflections on the mystery and meaning of suffering*, (Maryland: The Word among us Press, 2008), 13.

Reflection

*Whoever does not carry the cross and follow me
cannot be my disciple (Luke 14:27).
For to carry one's cross is to:
Be accountable for one's actions
Accept whatever life confronts us with
Know the weight of sin and suffering
Understand what turmoil is
Experience the injustices and hurts that enter life
Learn endurance and perseverance
Become stronger
Get on with life as best one can, despite limitations
Become more merciful towards the pressing needs of others
And see the source of suffering as a means
to new perspectives on life.
Only in our varied experiences of life, God,
can we really know our capacities and inner strengths,
Can we truly experience your unbounded compassion,
Do we really become a person of deep wisdom,
profound compassion
And wider understanding.
Then we become true carers to others. Amen.*

Chapter 8: Times of crises

> Therefore I am content with weaknesses, insults, hardships, persecutions, and calamities for the sake of Christ; for whenever I am weak, then I am strong. **- 2 Corinthians 12:10**
>
> Humpty Dumpty sat on a wall, Humpty Dumpty had a great fall, all the king's horses and all the king's men, couldn't put Humpty together again. The truth is that once you have broken an egg, all you can do is to make an omelette . . . unless the egg hasn't just been broken but has hatched! The secret is to trust that this may be so and then engage with the task of helping birth the new out of the shards of the old.[98]

Turning to the Scriptures

In the very beginning of the Bible, we read about Creation in Genesis 1:2 - 'The earth was a formless void and darkness covered the face of the deep, while a wind from God swept over the face of the waters.' Margaret Silf writes in reference to this verse that there is God's Spirit, energy, sweeping, erupting and foaming forth, similar to inside oneself, especially in the midst of flux, emptiness and darkness. What might happen with this raw material if one could let the Spirit hover? A wind of change can blow across the dark void; a new energy can emerge or even erupt; new possibilities can 'foam forth'; this is the singular gift of existence, forever renewing itself.[99] A lesson for us is that hope always hovers around us, no matter the crisis.

In the Christian Scriptures, if we are to take Jesus as our role model, we can better understand how to care for those facing crises. Jesus came face to face with difficult situations including the man with an unclean spirit (Mark 1:21-28, Luke 4:31-37), the feeding of the 5000 and 4000 (Matthew 14:13-21, Matthew 15:32-39, Mark 6:30-44, Mark 8:1-10, Luke 9:10-17, John 6:1-14), the sinful woman forgiven (Luke 7:36-

---
[98]Margaret Silf, *The other side of chaos. Breaking through when life is breaking down*, (Chicago: Loyola Press, 2011), 16-17.
[99]ibid, 44-45.

50), the Gerasene demoniac (Mark 5:1-20, Luke 8:26-39) and Gadarene demoniacs (Matthew 8:28-34), the boy with a demon (Matthew 17:14-20, Mark 9:14-29), demoniac mute man (Matthew 9:32-34), rejection at Nazareth (Matthew 13:54-58, Mark 6:1-6), unbelief of brothers (John 7:1-9), wedding at Cana (John 2:1-11), coming persecutions (Matthew 10:16-42), confronting a woman caught in adultery (John 8:1-10), cleansing the Temple (John 2:13-22), and stilling a storm (Mark 4:35-41, Mark 6:45-52, John 6:16-21).

There is never a stunned, helpless response from Jesus, in a crisis situation. Jesus assists those who struggle by his confident reassurance that the matter at hand can be transformed. So from these accounts we learn that ministry with people in crises includes:

- Removing shame
- Respecting the one before us
- Giving a voice to the voiceless
- Showing gentleness
- Ensuring safety is a priority
- Forgiveness
- Sense of being loved
- Being non judgmental
- Encouragement
- Non retaliation
- Non violence
- Peaceful acceptance

Jesus also dealt with his own crises including the temptation in the desert (Matthew 4:1-11), Judas' betrayal and Peter's denial (Matthew 26:69-75), Gethsemane (Matthew 26:36-46, Mark 14:32-52), his arrest (Luke 22:39-46) and death by crucifixion.

In John 21:15-19, Peter had denied Jesus three times just before the crucifixion. He had to live with his guilt from that moment onwards. Not only was he left mourning the death of a dear friend, he was also battling with his own sense of guilt and shame. He had hit rock bottom.

When the resurrected Jesus appears, he focuses his attention on Peter. Thrice he questions whether Peter loves him. This was not because Jesus ever doubted Peter's love. The questions were an opportunity for Peter to proclaim out loud what he failed to do the night before the crucifixion.

Jesus remains in Peter's presence, offering warmth, companionship, forgiveness and love. He restores Peter's self-worth and honours his dignity. And once Peter can look Jesus in the face again, Jesus encourages him to be the leader he was called to be. It is a reminder that we belong to God, no matter our failings and fears. Jesus offers us hope to get out of our darkness, to trust in our goodness, and to move forward in grace.

Crises faced today

Today, much of pastoral care, which was previously undertaken by 'religious' figures, is now taken up by others, including:
- individuals
- communities
- health care professionals
- family members
- friends
- neighbours
- organisations
- parishes

They are called to take on the roles of:
- spiritual director
- companion
- advocate
- theologian
- ethicist
- counsellor
- guide

- helping hand

Some of the kinds of life situations that can be helped by offering pastoral care today include:

- crisis care
- physical, psychological or sexual violence
- domestic violence
- depression
- post-traumatic stress disorder
- anxiety disorders
- alcohol and drug problems
- compulsive behaviours
- prison inmates
- family and marriage assistance
- relationship breakdown
- homelessness
- rape victims
- refugees and asylum seekers
- chronic pain
- physical disability
- loss
- suicide of someone dear
- unexpected change in life circumstances
- victims of bullying and harassment
- loss of meaning in life
- spiritual searching
- LGBTI
- sick
- elderly
- dying
- bereaved

Approaching someone in need of pastoral care requires human, relational, ethical and pastoral skills as it embraces care at the physical, mental, spiritual and social levels.

Religion as a coping mechanism

Results of more than two hundred published studies of religion's impact on physical health show the positive effect of religious involvement, through religious attendance, belief in God, religious experience, or frequent prayer. Religion may produce these salutary effects in a variety of ways:[100]

- Religious commitment is usually associated with lower rates of smoking, drinking and drug abuse behaviours
- Religious participation can act as a social support network
- Religious worship and prayer engender positive emotional experiences, such as relaxation, hope, forgiveness and love
- Religious faith may lead to optimism about one's health, trusting that God looks after all aspects of life
- Spirituality can promote a positive worldview and make sense of difficult situations
- Promoting other-directedness and forgiveness, thankfulness and hope
- Providing input in terms of ethical decision-making and moral dilemmas
- Sacramental offering and prayer give peace of mind

Religious involvement, personal faith, and spirituality have positive effects for a majority of people who turn to religious resources to cope with life and should be encouraged in pastoral care encounters.

Marcelo Saad and Roberta de Medeiros have noted that a well-constructed belief structure is a source of comfort, welfare, security, meaning, idealism and force. Many patients use their beliefs when coping with crisis. In contrast, a dysfunctional belief system may result in negative reactions that harm the healthcare evolution. These may be expressed through:[101]

---

[100] James Gollnick, *Religion and Spirituality in the Life Cycle*, (NY: Peter Lang, 2008), 217.
[101] Marcelo Saad and Roberta de Medeiros Chapter 7 'Spiritual-Religious Coping – Health Services Empowering Patients' Resources' in *Complementary Therapies for the Contemporary Healthcare*. Intech. Open science. Open minds. Year 2012 Pages 133-135.

- Attempt to bargain for recovery
- Belief of being deservedly affected (Low Self Worth)
- Diminished sense of meaning and purpose (Demotivation)
- Guilt, Confusion, Religious Stigmas (Disruption)
- Sorrow, Betrayal, Anger towards God (Disappointment)
- Subtle perception of vulnerability and finitude (Fear)
- Naïve reliability on religion omnipotence
- Sudden turn to unusual religious practices
- Dependency on religious leaders
- Obsessive ritualistic behaviour
- Sectarianism, Isolation, Fanaticism
- Refuse certain kinds of treatment

A pastoral carer needs to be aware of these expressions and gently direct the person towards a clearer interpretation of the situation, to help ease their unsettled minds.

When a care seeker can effectively use spiritual and religious practices to cope with a crisis, it will become an ongoing resource in maintaining and deepening a connection with God and a sense of life as sacred. The victims will be able to construct religious meanings and spiritual practices that are personally relevant and enhance a sense of their ability to be in charge of their lives.[102]

A pastoral care response to crises

In finding oneself in a situation where the person is facing a crisis and there is no healthy way of coping, then they will respond to a trigger event by acting in violent ways that were modelled to them in formative experiences. After the explosion of the abuse, there may be intense remorse, or denial and emotional shutdown. The cycle may become repetitive. Generally, these symptoms are normal reactions and are part of the natural healing process. With understanding and support from family and friends, the symptoms usually resolve more rapidly. Ways a pastoral carer can assist those experiencing a crisis include:

---

[102]Doehring, *The Practice of Pastoral Care: A Postmodern Approach*, 135.

- Be available
- Listen compassionately as someone tells their story
- Acknowledge and honour the story
- Create a 'safe space' – if there is any indication of violence, then caregivers must ensure the safety of the victim and whether mandatory reporting is required. Once physical safety is assured, pastoral caregivers can help victims establish a sense of psychological safety by assessing the extent to which victims are re-experiencing memories in nightmares, anxiety attacks, or flashbacks, and how they cope with these experiences.[103]
- Try to understand the feelings and perspective of the person
- Help them to tune into their feelings and work out what they need
- Support the person in exploring and developing realistic plans and solutions to keep themselves safe
- Walk with them and assist them to see real changes in their life. This means making small steps in the beginning
- Encouraging them to assume as much responsibility as possible for their own welfare
- Enlist the help of family and friends to assist in supporting the person
- Encourage them to utilise professional supports available

People in crises need to accept they are vulnerable and are suffering. They need assistance to search for ways to solve their problems. A pastoral carer can assist them to find resources and help. People facing crises need to be given the capacity to assess the situations correctly and know what to do next, that is the ability to protect themselves.

Aside from accompaniment, the pastoral carer can suggest the following practical exercises to assist those who have experienced crisis:

- Go for a walk
- Do a relaxation exercise
- Relax

---

[103]Doehring, *The Practice of Pastoral Care*: A Postmodern Approach, 139.

- Take a hot bath
- Spend time with a pet
- Sit in a sacred place
- Write a journal entry
- Play a musical instrument
- Listen to music
- To heal the trauma of war, the horror needs to be put into words, so it can be organised and talked about. Then step by step, by working it out verbally, one can reclaim their place in humanity explains Jean-Paul Mari.[104]
- Paint - Melissa Walker notes that art-making accesses the same sensory areas of the brain that encodes trauma. When service members create masks, it allows them to come to grips, literally, with their trauma, and enables them to break through and start to heal.[105]
- Provision of material needs
- Opportunities to be creative
- Religious and spiritual practices like prayer and worship
- Sacraments
- Reading the Scriptures

Margaret Silf offers - in the midst of transition - a few practical ideas as one navigates the rapids of crises:[106]

- Live primarily in the new mind-set
- Approach the transition by viewing it primarily as a birth, not a death
- Maintain a creatively critical stance toward the transition
- Give yourself time to catch up with the speed of change

---

[104] Jean-Paul Mari, *The chilling aftershock after a brush with death*
http://www.ted.com/talks/jean_paul_mari_the_chilling_aftershock_of_a_brush_with_death/transcript?language=en

[105] Melissa Walker: Art can heal PTSD's invisible wounds
http://www.ted.com/talks/melissa_walker_art_can_heal_ptsd_s_invisible_wounds/transcript?language=en

[106] Silf, *The other side of chaos. Breaking through when life is breaking down*, 152-157

- Reflect on the legacy of anything you have lost or had to leave behind
- Shed baggage
- Accept responsibility for what happens to your life
- Allow yourself to grieve for your losses
- Face your fears
- Focus on the deepest centre, the core of your being
- Envision the future as you would like it to become
- Seek and nourish community

The homeless

Providing a warm and comforting meal for those in need is much more than just providing food. Usually they're very hungry and it might be their only meal for the day, but many homeless who come to soup vans come because they're experiencing great loneliness and emptiness inside. Most come to talk, or for assistance. These people may not attend other services during the day - as Danusia Kaska explains - as they feel ashamed, because they aren't adequately dressed, or haven't had a shower, so they come knowing at soup vans they will be accepted as they are.[107]

The chronically homeless are the most resistant to social services and other help and most likely to have substance abuse or mental health problems. Erin McCrory notes, 'They've told us that once your reality becomes eating out of garbage cans and you don't hear your name spoken for months at a time, you accept this is your reality . . . Their spirits are broken and they are lacking in hope and faith in people.'[108] One of the most tragic aspects of life is the inner demoralisation of people caught in the poverty trap. They are made to feel they have no worth, no say, nothing to contribute, and nothing they can do to effect change. One of the greatest services is to listen and to encourage them

---

[107]Danusia Kaska, 'Homelessness has many faces,' 19 June 2017. https://www.eurekastreet.com.au/article.aspx?aeid=52594#.WUhRvmiGOU
[108]What do you say to a homeless person? Advice from Catholic urban missionaries. Catholic News Agency (CNA) Denver, Colo., Sep 23, 2016.
http://www.catholicnewsagency.com/news/what-do-you-say-to-a-homeless-person-advice-from-catholic-urban-mission aries-13851/1

to express themselves in their own way. So ways once can offer care to the homeless include:
- Greet the person
- Ask the person's name and remember it – the homeless go for months without hearing their own name
- Reach out and offer a handshake - this simple gesture breaks a barrier and expresses that you recognise their dignity.
- Spend time listening to their stories
- Love and compassion are appreciated
- Offer them some say in the ordering of their lives
- Pray with and for them

Practical means to offer help for the homeless include:
- People on the street often have teeth problems - soft foods like bananas are more edible
- Gift cards can be a better alternative to cash
- Give practical items like socks, water or gloves
- Items showing personal care are more likely to keep a focus on friendship
- In the winter months, warm clothing and shoes can go a long way

Homosexuality

There is no consensus about the social or genetic factors involved in the construction of sexual identity and orientation. As the American Psychological Association states:

> There is no consensus among scientists about the exact reasons that an individual develops a heterosexual, bisexual, gay or lesbian orientation. Although much research has examined the possible genetic, hormonal, developmental, social and cultural influences on sexual orientation, no findings have emerged that permit scientists to conclude that sexual orientation is determined by any particular factor or factors. Many think that nature and nurture both play complex roles; most people experience little or no sense of choice about their sexual orientation.[109]

---

[109] American Psychological Association: What causes a person to have a particular sexual orientation? http://www.apa.org/topics/lgbt/orientation.aspx

There is much pain, anger and misunderstanding behind the question, 'Do you think homosexuality is a sin?' All, regardless of sexual orientation, need to be enabled to love and accept oneself and to experience the unconditional love of God.

The church needs to find a way to honour the experience of gay people who are sincerely trying to live in accord with the gospel and the best wisdom of Catholic morality. As Pope Francis says:

> In Buenos Aires, I used to receive letters from homosexual persons who are 'socially wounded' because they tell me that they feel like the church has always condemned them. But the church does not want to do this. During the return flight from Rio de Janeiro, I said that if a homosexual person is of good will and is in search of God, I am no one to judge. By saying this, I said what the catechism says. Religion has the right to express its opinion in the service of the people, but God in creation has set us free: it is not possible to interfere spiritually in the life of a person . . . A person once asked me, in a provocative manner, if I approved of homosexuality. I replied with another question: 'Tell me: when God looks at a gay person, does he endorse the existence of this person with love, or reject and condemn this person?' We must always consider the person. Here we enter into the mystery of the human being. In life, God accompanies persons, and we must accompany them, starting from their situation. It is necessary to accompany them with mercy.[110]

A pastoral carer who believes that homosexual orientation necessitates a calling to celibacy still needs to be pastorally sensitive to the reality of the homosexual person's journey of life and faith. Ways the church can offer pastoral care for the LGBTI include:

- Cultivate an environment where people who experience same-sex attraction can talk
- Listen to their stories
- Be willing to engage with the truth of their experience
- Put homophobia to death in the parish

---

[110] Antonio Spadaro, 'A Big Heart Open to God. The exclusive interview with Pope Francis' in *Thinking Faith. The online Journal of British Jesuits.* www.thinkingfaith.org 19th September 2013.

- Educate others about the complexities of homosexuality
- Assure them they are loved by the church
- Give time to be with them
- Be sensitive to the pastoral needs of the parents, children and siblings

Reflection

The horror silences one
The injustices angers one
The violence is too graphic
The abuse is destructive
The hate consumes
The loss devastates.
There are many circumstances that leave one empty
of the will to hope
And the purpose of this life has no answer.
Things happen that shouldn't.
How, God, do we help when there is no hope?
Yet it is into such darkness and despair we are called.
We must enter the belly of the whale
And pull out into the light what we can salvage.
We cannot leave others in darkness
For then what is our purpose in life?
You called us to be 'the light of the world' (Matthew 5:14)
for this very reason –
So that hope may always prevail
So that evil won't have the final say.
So despite the waves of chaos that threaten to overwhelm
We continue to carry God's love and light
To refuse to become consumed by darkness.
We live in the light
And we believe, no matter . . .
No matter the troubles and woes.
We are meant for God
We are children of God
We are messengers of Good News
We are the light to others
The hope that makes life worth living
The care that reaches out and dives deep
To snatch others from the snares of destruction
And bring them into the warmth of God's love.

*We care because we believe
Everyone deserves the best that life can offer.
God's grace is always with us
To find a way for love to rise and reclaim. Amen.*

Chapter 9: Care of the young

> Jesus was frequently called a teacher. . . A good teacher has a genuine love for each student, takes each student exactly as he or she is at any given time, encourages all students to believe in themselves and in their ability to learn, creates in them enthusiasm and the desire to move forward, and seeks to bring out their best. Whenever necessary, the good teacher consoles and reassures, but at other times seeks greater effort from a student. – **Geoffrey Robinson**[111]

Jesus as role model

If we are to take Jesus as our role model, we can better understand how to care for the young. Jesus blesses the little children who were brought to him (Luke 18:15-17), he raised Jairus' twelve-year-old daughter (Luke 8:40-56), he told the parable of the two sons (Matthew 21:28-32), and the parable of the prodigal son (Luke 15:11-32), he healed a boy with a demon (Luke 9:37-43), and he healed the Syro-Phoenician woman's daughter (Mark 7:24-30).

In the account where Jesus blesses the little children (Mark 10:13-16), 'he took them up in his arms, laid his hands on them, and blessed them' (10:16). Jesus delights in the young, for they are a joy to the heart and bring a smile to the face. They are not a nuisance because they disrupt our routine with their noisy fanfare. They are in Jesus' eyes precious and models of truth, as he notes, 'it is to such as these that the kingdom of God belongs' (10:14). They are who they are, with their innocence, love and need for attention and care. Jesus offers them acceptance and defends their rights in the face of those who want to fiercely hold them back. When 'the disciples spoke sternly' (10:13) Jesus became 'indignant' (10:14) and embraced the children with love. It is our choice to offer them our time and blessing, to encourage them into their full potential. The young thrive on attention and love, and adults must create that welcoming space. Jesus showed that rather than be about disciplining the young, it is about discipling them.

---

[111]Geoffrey Robinson, *Travel in Sacred Places*, p. 22.

From these encounters of Jesus with the young, we learn that ministry with young people includes:
- Welcoming them
- Enjoying their company
- Nourishing them
- Spending time with them
- Conversing
- Healing
- Restoring
- Forgiveness
- Loving
- Offering them responsibility
- Offering new ways of living
- Challenging their lifestyles and choices
- Creating a safe place
- Waiting patiently
- Trusting their judgment
- Accepting them no matter their background
- Extending a helping hand
- Restoring dignity
- Removing shame, affliction and disgrace
- Returning them home

Youth Issues

Growing up is a complicated time for the young. They are juggling body changes, erratic emotions, navigating relationships, peer pressure, societal expectations, family issues, bullying, loneliness, addictions, lack of role models, unemployment, sexuality, stress of school life, study, exams, holding a job and proving their man/womanhood. On days, they soar high, followed by pessimistic moods, hiding in dark places. Sometimes, they enjoy an adrenaline rush, but at other times, they sit and complain, with self-pity. They are searching for a sense of belonging, an experience of God, a spiritual encounter that offers hope and comfort, healing and security, assurance and wonder.

Unfortunately, adults do use power to manipulate the young to think and behave like they want them to. The young become targets for:

- Advertising companies
- Paedophiles
- Radicalisation
- Consumer markets
- Alcohol and drugs lords
- Gang and crime syndicates
- Sexualisation

How can the young come to know their value is much more than their possessions, their images, their popularity?

The 2016 Mission Australia Youth survey[112] provides insight into the world of the young. Friendships, family relationships and school or study satisfaction ranked as the three most highly valued items, followed by physical and mental health. Top issues of personal concern were coping with stress, school or study problems and body image followed by depression and family conflict.

Top three sources of help for young people were friend/s, parent/s and relatives/family friends. Other sources included brother/sister, internet, teacher or school counsellor. Majority of respondents were positive in regards to family's ability to get along.

Most important issues in Australia in 2016 were alcohol and drugs, equity and discrimination and mental health. Since 2014, international relations and crime, safety and violence, have been increasingly identified as key issues facing the nation.

Top three activities for young people were sports (as a participant), sports (as a spectator) and volunteer work. Two thirds of respondents feel positive about the future.

---

[112]Bailey, V., Baker, A-M., Cave, L., Fildes, J., Perrens, B., Plummer, J. and Wearring, A. 2016, *Mission Australia's 2016 Youth Survey Report, Mission Australia*. 2016, p. 4.
https://www.missionaustralia.com.au/publications/research/young-people

Pastoral care

It is important to understand young people's journey to independence in order to determine the types of support they may require. Mission Australia provides services that aim to achieve the following outcomes for young people:[113]

- Developing and achieving – young people need to be skilled and confident, in education and with access to tertiary education, training or employment.
- Economic wellbeing –access to the essentials in life and good financial management skills. They should have pathways to economic participation, fulfilling employment and independent living.
- Healthy – being healthy includes participating in activities such as sport. Health incorporates both physical and mental health.
- Housed – a supportive and stable home environment is a particularly important aspect of a young person's life
- Inclusive and cohesive – having a strong sense of being included, having mutual support and feeling you have someone to call on at a time of need are critically important.
- Connected and participating – have a sense of belonging, feel part of the community and are given opportunities to participate in activities and events that allow them to develop relationships with others. Young people should have their voices heard and be actively involved in decisions affecting their lives.
- Safe – Young people need to feel safe in their families, communities and schools.
- Supported and resourced – young people and those around them such as their peers, family and relatives must have access to services to meet their needs.

In July 2009, the Australian Catholic Bishops Conference released a document titled *Anointed and Sent. An Australian Vision for Catholic*

---

[113]Bailey, V., Baker, A-M., Cave, L., Fildes, J., Perrens, B., Plummer, J. and Wearring, A. 2016, *Mission Australia's 2016 Youth Survey Report, Mission Australia.* 2016, p. 5.
https://www.missionaustralia.com.au/publications/research/young-people

Youth Ministry with a second edition in 2014.[114] It set out 3 goals and 8 focus areas that parishes should focus on in order to nourish the spirituality, vitality and faith of young people. One of the 8 focus areas was on pastoral care:

> Pastoral care is fundamentally a relationship: a compassionate presence, modelled on Jesus' care for people, especially those hurting and in need, and nurturing their growth toward wholeness. Young people need such care and are in turn called to actively care for others. This requires a higher order of authentic relationship and maturity. Pastoral care guides young people in their emotional-spiritual development and accompanies them as they build moral character and discern their vocation. It equips them to deal practically and prayerfully with life situations, fostering the link between faith and decision-making. It promotes life-giving choices, including those around sexuality, relationships, life-plans and problem-solving. Pastoral care involves compassionate outreach, loving each individual in their situation. It requires personal support for and by young people, especially listening in a spirit of companionship. It requires regular access to sacraments of Reconciliation and Eucharist. Pastoral care creates networks of support for young people in times of crisis and beyond. It provides direct aid to youth at risk, promotes development of communication and other life skills, and links services in the wider community.

So how does one pastorally care for the young:

- Greet and welcome them
- Visit, affirm, invite
- Remember names – it communicates something very special, their identity
- Listen in a spirit that encourages expression of thoughts and feelings
- Pay attention to them
- Make them feel good about themselves

---

[114] Australian Catholic Bishops Conference, *Anointed and Sent. An Australian Vision for Catholic Youth Ministry*, Second Edition, 2014 http://evangelisationbrisbane.org.au/assets/uploads/anointed-and-sent.pdf

- Encourage communication around sexuality, problem solving and relationships
- Treat young people as individuals
- Provide room/space where they can feel comfortable
- Be open
- Acknowledge their suffering, anger, depression, dreams, illusions, and lack of confidence
- Address factors including poverty, discrimination and special needs
- Encourage their light, hope and possibility for growth
- Empower them into leadership positions
- Involve them in decision making and goal setting
- Provide opportunities for personal growth and to develop self-esteem
- Offer ethical guidance and values
- Provide immersion experiences
- Be positive and liberal with praise, compassion, grace
- Engage their families
- Provide variety, interest and challenge
- Role modelling
- Talk over their ideas and views
- Serve them
- Pray for them and their requests
- Create networks of support for young people, communities and families
- Provide direct aid to youth at risk

As young people find themselves in a western worldview characterised by individualism and secularism, the church community is called to be a collective cultural system, a place of belonging, and a place where spirituality is nurtured. Pastoral care by the church towards the young needs to:

- Ensure congruence between their beliefs and real life experiences
- Uphold family values
- Support cultural practices
- Ritual observances
- Engage in social issues of today

Ways to care for students in schools

Young people learn attitudes and behaviour from what significant others such as parents, teachers and peers, reinforce for them. Religious educators in classrooms are then, first called to witness to Christ, to be disciples. However, Frances M. Moran notes that the approach to students is not always positive. He describes two ways of viewing students:

The student as **object** - results are what schools look for today. This is what parents pay for. Standards of literacy and numeracy are aimed ultimately at employment in the marketplace. The current climate is one of fierce competition between schools. Bright students and outstanding athletes are poached from one school to another as are teachers who are considered 'good at getting results.' Consequently, students today are commodified objects. They become a statistic that reveals a school's position in terms of success ratings. Not surprisingly many students feel lost in big schools, others gain individual attention through the presentation of various problems, while others stand out as achievers – along market lines.[115]

The student as **subject** - pastoral practice focuses on the notion of subjectivity and so each and every student matters. It is not aimed only at those in trouble. It is a practice conducted in numerous and diverse contexts, most especially for those students whose voice is rarely heard. They are the many students who pass by unnoticed because they fit the system. Yet they are the students most at risk of commodification or objectification. Pastoral practice is not problem-centered but rather subject or life-centred. It is the teachers' role to consider the students as subjects, persons who are more than their academic and sporting abilities though inclusive of these as well.[116]

---

[115]Frances M. Moran, *Beyond the culture of care. Helping those souled-out by the market economy*, (NSW: St Pauls, 2006), 86-91.
[116]ibid, 91.

Pastoral care becomes the role of all teachers, parents and support staff along with all students. Its scope is wide enough to include the social, educational, mental, emotional and physical dimensions, and utilises the best in research to ensure the needs of the young are met. In a Western Australian study on pastoral care in education, some of the key findings emerging from the review of best practice included:[117]

- A clearly articulated and comprehensive pastoral care policy
- A health culture that promotes student connectedness
- A relevant, engaging and stimulating curriculum which is linked with the broader community and global context
- Effective and productive pedagogies
- A democratic, empowering and positive classroom management approach
- Well established internal and external support structures and networks
- An alternative flexible learning environment

Well-developed pastoral care policies in schools incorporate not just the spiritual care of students but also provide early intervention for at-risk groups, and intervention for special needs groups, as well as individual casework to resolve existing problems and encourage re-integration.

---

[117]*Pastoral Care in Education* Prepared for: Department of Education and Training Western Australia Prepared by: Child Health Promotion Research Unit Edith Cowan University March 2006 http://www.det.wa.edu.au/studentsupport/behaviourandwellbeing/detcms/cms-service/download/asset/?asset_id=8272773

Reflection

In this fast and busy world with so much going on
Little people, young ones, need a sense of security and safety
To know they belong and are wanted
To be loved and to love back.

The young will not always be young.
They are growing and becoming
So in the process may they encounter:
Parental love to know no matter what,
they are important to someone
Friendships to learn trust
Relationships to know that life is about others too
Community to feel belonging and support
Encouragement to continue on
Values to develop their character
Wisdom in decision making
Help so they can get up and move on
Laughter to open them up to life
Opportunities to develop their potential
Possibilities to engage in new experiences
Adventure to enjoy the here and now
Employment to feel a sense of contribution
Beauty in order to appreciate what is given
Struggle to gain courage and hope
Care to be able to empathise with others
Generosity to give of their time to others
Love to grow in its warmth
Spirituality to awaken them to mystery
God to really know who they are. Amen.

Chapter 10: Care of the elderly

What Do You See, Nurse?
What do you see, nurse, what do you see?
What are you thinking when you look at me?
A crabbed old woman, not very wise,
uncertain of habit with faraway eyes?
Who dribbles her food and makes no reply?
When you say in a loud voice, 'I do wish you'd try.'
Who seems not to notice the things that you do
and forever is losing a stocking or shoe?
Who, resisting or not, lets you do as you will
with bathing and feeding, the long day to fill?
Is that what you're thinking, is that what you see?
Then open your eyes; you're not looking at me.
I'll tell you who I am as I sit here so still
as I move at your bidding, as I eat at your will.
I am a small child with a father and mother,
brothers and sisters who love one another.
A young girl of sixteen with wings at her feet,
dreaming that soon now a lover she'll meet.
A bride soon at twenty, my heart gives a leap,
remembering the vows that I promised to keep.
At twenty-five, now I have young of my own,
who need me to build a secure, happy home.
A woman of thirty, my young now grow fast,
bound to each other with ties that should last.
At forty, my young now soon will be gone,
but my man stays beside me to see I don't mourn.
At fifty, once more babies play around my knee.
Again, we know children, my loved one and me.
Dark days are upon me, my husband is dead.
I look at the future, I shudder with dread.
For my young are all busy rearing young of their own

and I think of the years and the love I have known.
I'm an old lady now and nature is cruel,
'tis her jest to make old age look like a fool.
The body it crumbles, grace and vigour depart
and now there's a stone where I once had a heart.
But inside this old carcass, a young girl still dwells
and now and again my battered heart swells.
I remember the joys, I remember the pain,
and I am loving and living life over again.
I think of the years all too few, gone so fast
and accept the stark fact that nothing can last.
Open your eyes, nurse, open and see
not a crabbed old woman, look closer - see me.[118]

My Father Began as a God - Ian Mudie

My father began as a god, full of heroic tales of days when he was young. His ways were as immutable as if brought down from Sinai, which indeed he thought they were. He fearlessly lifted me to heaven by a mere swing to his shoulder and made of me a godling by seating me astride our milch-cow's back, and, too, upon a great white gobbler of which others went in constant fear. Strange then how he shrank and shrank until by my time of adolescence he had become a foolish small old man with silly and outmoded views of life and of morality. Stranger still that as I became older his faults and his intolerances scaled away into the past, revealing virtues such as honesty, generosity, integrity. Strangest of all how the deeper he recedes into the grave the more I see myself as just one more of all the little men who creep through life not knee-high to this long-dead god.[119]

---

[118] Phyliss McCormick, 'Crabbit Old Woman' http://mrmom.amaonline.com/stories/CrabbitOldWoman.htm

[119] Ian Mudie, 'My Father began as a God' https://fundos.wikispaces.com/file/view/My+Father+Began+as+a+God.pdf

From Scripture

In the Gospels, we read of a number of events where Jesus encounters the elderly including Simon's mother-in-law (Matthew 8:14-17, Mark 1:29-34, Luke 4:38-41), a woman crippled for eighteen years (Luke 13:10-17) and the healing of an invalid man at the pool at Bethzatha (John 5:1-9).

In reflecting on the elderly woman who had been crippled for eighteen years, she entered the synagogue, unfaltering in her faith despite being 'quite unable to stand up straight' (Luke 13:11). She elicits a response of compassion from Jesus, who desires to be part of the lives of the elderly. Jesus lays 'his hands on her' (13:13), blessing, consecrating, connecting, offering a warm gesture that leads to healing and wholeness. Tenderly, Jesus cares for the fragile elderly, compassionately he looks upon them, and lovingly he cares.

In response, the elderly crippled woman immediately 'stood up straight and began praising God' (Luke 13:13). Restored to fullness of life, there was no bitterness for the past struggles, but only joyful anticipation of the future ahead. Like so many elderly, who are given a new lease on life, she was ready 'to face the world' courageously, ever mindful that God walks among us.

Jesus publicly demonstrates that his healing love is for all and opposes the culture of indifference and apathy displayed by the religious leader in the passage. Proper response is always meant to be one of compassion and mercy, in particular for the elderly, who often find themselves alone, unnoticed and unwanted.

Ageing

Gerontological research shows considerable continuity in the personality from adulthood into old age with continued earlier patterns of thought, emotion, and behaviour, spirituality and implicit religion of midlife. However, physical and mental disabilities may precipitate substantial personality changes as James Gollnick explains.[120] The aging process involves:

---

[120] James Gollnick, *Religion and Spirituality in the Life Cycle*, (NY: Peter Lang, 2008), 211.

- Physical changes - no peak performance, bodily changes, loss of sight and hearing, medical treatment, loss of flexibility in joints, slower recovery from exertion or illness, increase in chronic illnesses, get more tired, etc.
- Psychological effects – mental abilities and personalities remain remarkably stable throughout the life span although they can slow down.
- Social change – roles, relationships, occupational status, retirement, relocation, death of a spouse and close friends.
- Spiritual changes - sadness and sorrows of life, grieving, adjusting, compensating and rebuilding. Life experience of God's presence and love provides a sense of trust and hope.

Erik Erikson characterises the final stage of life as ego-integrity versus despair and disgust. The main achievement in this process is to accept one's life as something that had to be, even with its limitations and failures. If the elderly person is unable to reach a degree of emotional integration, despair develops around the realisation that sufficient time and energy no longer remain for building something that seems 'right.' Coming to terms with failures and missed opportunities as well as accomplishments requires the elderly to experience a range of positive and negative emotions on their way to ego-integrity.[121]

Disengagement Theory

The disengagement theory argues that older people develop different values than the young, leading them to become less emotionally involved in activities and relationships that occupied them in the middle ages. They disengage from their social roles as their place in society and their health diminishes. Society reinforces this withdrawal through lack of interest in, and opportunities for the elderly, but essentially disengagement is seen as a natural rather than an imposed process.[122]

Where companies, advertisers and culture insist life is to be lived with adrenaline rush, exotic holidays, latest technologies, current fashion, fine dining, etc, the elderly are not drawn into the hype. What

[121] ibid, 219-220.
[122] ibid, 211.

appears as a necessity to younger generations are only fads to the elderly. They have passed through temptations, fortune and pleasure. They now seek their own space, pursue their own choices, and their own deeper needs.

The elderly should have time to reflect on their experience and attend to their inner lives after years of pressure to conform to occupational and social roles. However, it is important, that through disengagement, the elderly do not remain focused on the negative features of their world, which may include:

- Decline in hearing and seeing
- Decline in their health and that of their loved ones
- Becoming disabled
- Dependent on others
- Lack strength and energy
- Memory weakens
- Loss of social status as productive workers
- Issues of safety and vulnerability to assault and robbery
- Declining finances
- Selling their homes and moving into aged care
- Boredom, depression and fear
- Lonely and a burden to their children
- Feel less able to face conflict
- Coping with loss and death of family and friends
- Widowhood
- Death is the ultimate challenge

Such negative features can undermine the ability and desire to remain active, with the majority of older people not taking advantage of available social opportunities such as senior centres.[123]

One of the tragic outcomes of loneliness is that people turn to television for consolation with two-fifths of older people reporting it is their principal company. So how does one assist those who are lonely?

---
[123] ibid, 207.

Australian Lifeline recommends that those suffering from loneliness, worthlessness, hopelessness, or thoughts of suicide, connect with friends and family, attend social functions, exercise, and get involved in the community.[124] Care for the ageing also includes:

- Addressing spiritual needs
- Dealing with illness, loss and bereavement
- Assisting the elderly to re-affirm integrity
- Attributing meaningful outcomes to physical or emotional suffering
- Discussing approaching death

In order for the elderly not to totally disengage from life, practical ways that a pastoral carer can assist include:

- Visit or phone on a regular basis
- Take them shopping
- Help them navigate the online world
- Help with difficult housework such as tidying cupboards, mopping floors, vacuuming
- Invite them to dinner
- Introduce them to social networks, with people of similar interests
- Encourage use of Skype to stay in touch with friends and family
- Bring gifts such as flowers or chocolates
- Arrange for a pedicure or massage
- Encourage gardening
- Gift them a pot plant that they can water and watch grow
- Spend time in the shed or kitchen with them
- Chat over a cup of tea
- Go for walks
- Take them to the doctors when need be
- Encourage them to help through sewing, fixing things for you, etc
- Seek their advice
- Listen to their life review of who they are and where they have been

---

[124] Loneliness Survey Finds Australians Are Very, Very Lonely – VICE
https://www.vice.com/en_au/article/loneliness-survey-finds-that-australians-are-very-lonely

- Share stories
- Discuss the latest news
- Take about life
- Take them to Mass
- Talk about faith

Getting active

Ageing is largely a positive experience and acquired coping skills enable one to generally function with effectiveness. Old age can be a journey towards communion and accepting weakness, rediscovering the beauty and simplicity of daily life. The more active older people are, the better mentally, physically and socially adjusted they are. Positive features of the world of the elderly include:

- More free time
- Fewer needs
- Acquired practical wisdom
- Surrounded by children and grandchildren
- More flexible
- Ready to be defined beyond work or the work role
- Not having the burden of holding a job with its demands
- A new sense of achievement at what their working life has done
- Involved in new interests
- Take delight in small everyday things
- Spending time with grandchildren
- Skyping distant family members
- Cooking for their families
- Discover their inner self
- Get philosophical
- Independence and the ability to provide for their own needs
- Free to break with convention and conformity

The elderly are aided when society assists older people to recover their identity as culture bearers and creators. Pope John Paul II emphasised the importance of the elderly in today's society:

> Elderly people help us to see human affairs with greater wisdom, because life's vicissitudes have brought them knowledge and maturity. They are the guardians of our collective memory, and thus the privileged interpreters of that body of ideals and common values which support and guide life in society. To exclude the elderly is in a sense to deny the past, in which the present is firmly rooted, in the name of a modernity without memory. Precisely because of their mature experience, the elderly are able to offer young people precious advice and guidance. [125]

The elderly continue to have a role to play in society, including evangelisation of grandchildren, instilling courage by their loving advice, silent prayers and patient witness of suffering.

Pope Francis describes older generations as 'the roots and memory of a people,' which make them 'a precious treasure.' He urged grandparents to 'talk to your grandchildren. Let them ask you questions.' In a world where 'strength and appearance are often idealised, you have the mission of witnessing to the values that truly count and that always remain.'[126]

As their life expectancy is limited, the elderly conceive of a future that is about what they care about, their relationships, marriage, children and grandchildren. They feel they contribute to their grandchildren's development and take pride. This connection to younger generations gives the elderly coherence.

Active participation of the elderly, combined with reflective withdrawal, allows for full self-actualisation, in moving beyond achievement and production, searching for something more through reflection. As Joan Chittister OSB writes in 'Growing Older Gracefully:'[127]

---

[125]Pope John Paul II Letter to the elderly, in 1999, paragraph 10. https://w2.vatican.va/content/john-paul-ii/en/letters/1999/documents/hf_jp-ii_let_01101999_elderly.html
[126]Pope Francis, 'Society marginalises the elderly' Address on 15 October 2016, *Catholic News Service*
http://www.catholicherald.co.uk/news/2016/10/17/society-is-marginalises-the-elderly-pope-tells-audience-of-grandparents/
[127]Joan Chittister OSB, 'Growing Older Gracefully' from *The Gift of Years* (2008) http://spirituality.ucanews.com/2014/10/13/growing-older-gracefully/

It is a very comforting feeling to know that age does not change us. On the contrary. In some ways, we are all just getting to be more of who and what we have always been. Which means, of course, that we can decide right now what we intend to be like when we're eighty: approachable and lovable, or tyrannous and fractious . . . We only get to be more of what we have always wanted to be. We are free now to choose the way we live in the world, the way we relate to the world around us, the attitudes we take to life, the meaning we get out of it, the gifts we put into it. And all of them can change . . .

Instead of honoring the wisdom and experience of the generations before us—as did the Greeks and the Romans and the American Indians, for instance—industrial/technological society infantilizes anyone whose life is no longer caught up in the skills and languages of that world. Once people can no longer talk about advertising plans or departmental goals or the job, the experience they garnered over the years is no longer a premium in the very society that produced it all. Instead, people grow useless by the end of the next quarterly report. Their so-called experience counts for nothing . . .

But freedom in old age is the ability to be the best of the self I have developed during all those years. It is the freedom to gather everything I have learned up to this point and to put it to even more exciting use now. It is the freedom to give myself away to those who really need me, in ways I have never had the chance of doing before. I am free to be important to people with real needs. And with that new role in life, I become one of those rare people who know what it takes to go through life, survive its dislocations, outlive its expectations, and negotiate its shoals. Now I am free to do it not simply for my own sake—but for the sake of the world at large.

. . . Now is the time to think it all through again. Everything. God, life, work, relationships, behaviors, goals. I am free now to measure all of them against my experience, to reshape them out of my new knowledge, to try things wherever my new spiritual energy leads me, to add new ideas to the old ideas that have controlled my life for so long.

Spending time with the elderly, engaging in conversation that illicit responses filled with vast experience, rich history and vivid memory, can be an enlightening time. A pastoral carer can ask the elderly about:
- What keeps them going in life?
- How they spend their time?
- How would they like to be remembered?
- What are they most proud of?
- What gives them most pleasure?
- How do they sense God?

Respect for the dignity of older persons and solidarity with them, requires fostering opportunities to participate in family, church and community life, and if possible, to live in their home environment. The church can offer counselling and social support programs. Churches can set up a seniors committee that can play important roles including:
- Visiting elderly in aged care
- Visiting elderly in their homes
- Encouraging the elderly to contribute by cooking, knitting etc. for church fetes, etc.
- Seniors Mass
- Monthly bus outings
- Monthly lunches and get together

Aged care facilities

The *Australian Code of Ethical Standards* states, 'Every effort should be made to ensure that institutional environments for older persons respect their individuality and are as homelike as possible. In addition to high quality nursing care and social services as required, special provision should be made for the spiritual needs of older persons.'[128] Specific challenges which aged care facilities have identified include:
- A number of residents don't have family members, leading to emotional pain.

---

[128] Code of Ethical Standards – Catholic Health Australia for Catholic Health and Aged Care Services in Australia, 4.4. http://www.stvincents.com.au/assets/files/pdf/CodeofEthicalStandards.pdf

- There are those who ignore their abilities and capacities, refusing to participate in the activities provided, due to lack of motivation, confidence and self-esteem.
- Their physical incapacities include inability to walk, eat, see or hear.

Specific initiatives to help the elderly maintain (or recover) a sense of hope:

- Maintain an optimum standard of nursing care and high quality service.
- Acknowledge and uphold the dignity of each resident. To this end, health is given with compassion, care, love and encouragement with every consideration for privacy and comfort.
- Ensure their spiritual, physical and emotional needs are met.
- Offer comfortable, secure, pleasant, clean, well-aired and bright surroundings and create an atmosphere of homeliness.
- Notify the residents about their right to exercise freedom of choice, to make their own decisions about personal aspects of daily life, financial affairs and possessions.
- Individuality of the residents is emphasised and respected both in the preparation of care planning and in the way that the staff perform their duties.
- Develop confidence, self-esteem and competence for self-improvement through activities such as attending local events, day trips, games, discussion, exercise groups, and BBQs.

The goals of aged care include promoting health and well-being. It should also ensure that the elderly have access to appropriate services which enable them as far as possible to recover health and to participate in family life, church and wider society. Such ministry must be done with love and compassion, mercy and care. It follows that staff must see themselves and the patients as forming an equivalent of a family system and maintaining an environment where they are able to discuss their hopes and fears, frustrations and joys.

Reflection

Our elderly, taking time with ease,
Teaching us to appreciate every moment,
Instead of entering into heedless rush.
We search for time to be with them,
While they wait and wait for us.
May we learn their patience
Their ever more accepting attitude to life,
Their delight in everyday things we take for granted,
Their appreciation of gardening, hobbies, quiet time.
We come to care, but they welcome us as friends
Opening their hearts to us,
Ready to tell, to give, to love.
They teach us to put down our defences,
to share who we really are
and to take a new perspective on life.
We pray to become like them,
Wise and appreciative of life. Amen.

Chapter 11: Care of the sick

A brother said to an old man: 'There are two brothers. One of them stays in his cell quietly fasting for six days at a time, and imposing on himself a good deal of discipline, and the other serves the sick. Which one of them is more acceptable to God?' The old man replied, 'Even if the brother who fasts six days were to hang himself by the nose, he could not equal the one who serves the sick.'[129]

The Scriptures

In turning to the Scriptures, there are numerous times in which Jesus is confronted with the sick. These include the healing of the leper (Matthew 8:1-4, Mark 1:40-45, Luke 5:12-16), paralytic (Matthew 9:1-8; Mark 2:1-12, Luke 5:17-26), man with a withered hand (Matthew 12:9-14, Mark 3:1-6, Luke 6:6-11), healing of the Centurion's servant (Matthew 8:5-13; Luke 7:1-10), healing an official's son (John 4:46-53), haemorrhaging woman (Matthew 9:18-26, Mark 5:25-34, Luke 8:43-48), man with dropsy (Luke 14:1-6), the ten lepers (Luke 17:11-19), blind man (Mark 8:22-26, John 9:1-12), the blind beggar Bartimaeus (Mark 11:46-52), Luke 18:35-43), two blind men (Matthew 9:27-31, Matthew 20:29-34), the sick in Gennesaret (Matthew 14:34-36, Mark 6:53-56), Canaanite woman's daughter (Matthew 15:21-28, Mark 7:24-30), deaf man (Mark 7:31-37), and many other cures (Matthew 15:29-31).

In focusing on the healing of the paralytic, Jesus is at home and the crowds flock to him (Mark 2:1-12). Then the scene shifts to 'some people' including 'four of them'. We don't know who they are but what we do know is that they desperately wanted the paralytic healed, that they climbed to the roof, dug through it, and brought down the paralytic on a stretcher.

---

[129] Joan Chittister, *In God's Holy Light: wisdom from the desert monasteries*, (Cincinatti: Franciscan Media, 2015), 11.

Jesus is amazed by their faith and turns his attention to the paralytic. We know the rest of the story but let us focus on the helpers. The love they had for this paralytic was so deep, they would go to any lengths to help him. It contrasts to today's society, where the physically dependent, mentally ill, or socially awkward, are shunned by society at large and considered a burden. A society where abortions and euthanasia are justified because the possible quality of life doesn't meet society's standards. This story is a reminder that we are called to support and be by the side of those most defenceless and vulnerable.

These people who surrounded the paralytic with love and concern enabled Jesus to heal the paralytic, and all are in need of such friends. The love and care of others goes a long way in helping heal minds and hearts.

Time and time again Jesus is healing the sick and allowing hope and forgiveness, for, as he says, 'Those who are well have no need of a physician, but those who are sick; I have come to call not the righteous but sinners' (Mark 2:17). Jesus' healing miracles were signs of the coming of God's Kingdom whose creative plan did not include sickness and death.

The quest for cures

Care of souls has its origins in the Latin *cura*. Commonly translated as care, it contains the idea of both care and *cure*. The church embraces both meanings of cura, understanding care to involve nurture and support, along with healing and restoration. The Christian community is there to offer a depth of spiritual and practical support and not just the hope of elusive and high-risk physical cures, as reflected in the scenario about Heinz who steals a drug:

> In Europe, a woman was near death from a special kind of cancer. There was one drug that the doctors thought might save her. It was a form of radium that a druggist in the same town had recently discovered. The drug was expensive to make, but the druggist was charging ten times what the drug cost him to make. He paid $200 for the radium and charged $2,000 for a small dose of the drug. The sick woman's husband, Heinz, went to everyone

he knew to borrow the money, but he could only get together about $1,000 which is half of what it cost. He told the druggist that his wife was dying and asked him to sell it cheaper or let him pay later. But the druggist said, 'No, I discovered the drug and I'm going to make money from it.' So Heinz got desperate and broke into the man's store to steal the drug for his wife. (Kohlberg, 1963, p. 19)

Hope in medicine can lead to an unrealistic expectation that medicine can cure any disease. So while doctors speak from a biomedical perspective, patients or families often speak from a religious one. The aim of both medicine and theology is to better understand the reason for human suffering and to seek ways to relieve it. As medicine is called upon to sustain life, theology can assist in exploring the meaning of life as well as avenues for spiritual healing.[130]

It is desirable to incorporate the roles of pastoral carer, physician and nurse as co-equals and collaborators. Physicians focus on the anatomical, physiological and diagnostic. Pastoral carers focus on guilt and reconciliation, suffering and meaning of illness, and the person's spiritual destiny and inner peace.

Pain control

Galen, a famous Greek physician, made the first discovery that pain, associated with the sensation of touch, was related to the central nervous system and brain function. However, it was Cicely Saunders who developed the concept of total pain that involves physical, mental, social and spiritual factors. This is captured in the English word *health* which is derived from the old Saxon word *hal*, from which we get *hale* and *whole*.

The word 'pain' originates from the Greek word *poine*, which means penalty, and the Latin word *poena* meaning punishment. This understanding of pain being caused by 'evil spirits' or 'punishment' by God, can be addressed with concepts of reconciliation, love and forgiveness, to alleviate any sense of guilt that may be affecting the person's healing.

---

[130] Abigail Rian Evans, 'Healing in the Midst of Dying: A Collaborative Approach to End-of-Life Care' in *Living well and dying Faithfully*, John Swinton and Richard Payne (ed.), (Grand Rapids, Michigan: William B. Eerdmans Publishing Company, 2009), 170.

One of the issues that a pastoral carer faces is over use or under use of drugs, in controlling pain, by patients or families. *The Catholic Health Code of Ethical Standards* states:

> Patients and residents have the primary responsibility for judging which treatment and care options serve their authentic good in the totality of their circumstances. When people are incapable of making their own decisions, their family, guardian or other legal representative and the senior doctor (or other relevant professional) have the responsibility of discerning what is in the patient's or resident's best interest, in the light of what is known of the patient's wishes.[131]

The patient's concerns

When a person is hospitalised, there is the suddenness of the event and the disruption to what was a normal everyday life. Naturally, what follows is an array of emotions that may be related to a number of factors such as:

- reason for admission
- difficulties in the health system
- lack of privacy
- anxiety
- fear
- visitors
- meals
- communication
- the disease
- diagnosis and treatment
- medical tests and procedures
- side effects of treatment
- pain, discomfort and loss of energy
- loss of control and independence

---

[131] Catholic Health Australia. Code of Ethical Standards for Catholic Health and Aged Care Services in Australia, 2001, no. 5.

- vulnerability
- isolation from the world
- care of family dependants
- work commitments
- coping with an uncertain future
- doubt the goodness of God
- the possibility of dying

People dealing with illness need to have appropriate control within their own life situations, and be able to find meaning in life. According to Frank Lopez, for those who can, their prime task, if they cannot get over their sickness, is to try to regain their lost or diminished humanness in some other way. The dignity and worth of each person is of greater value than the illness. Patients who are able to rethink their life as sick persons rather than think only of their past healthy existence can discover a new life with its own meaning.[132] The patient's search for power and control can involve:

- Looking for meaning in their experience of illness
- Learning to communicate more effectively with health professionals
- Ensuring they participate as far as possible in decision-making which concerns their care
- Research information to make informed judgments and maintain some control over decisions
- Investigate other ways of dealing with their illness
- Address personal and family issues
- Time for personal prayer and where possible attending religious services
- Make arrangements for death should that become a reality

Communication and information at each step can help patients understand how their illness is affecting them and what can be done to help. The reality is that healing is not only physical but spiritual, social and emotional as well, which comes through getting patients involved.

---

[132] Frank Lopez, *Applied Pastoral Care: A Contextual Approach*, 95.

Hospital chaplaincy

What do people who are sick and dying talk about with the chaplain? . . . Mostly, they talk about their families: about their mothers and fathers, their sons and daughters.
They talk about the love they felt, and the love they gave. Often they talk about love they did not receive, or the love they did not know how to offer, the love they withheld, or maybe never felt for the ones they should have loved unconditionally.
. . . People talk to the chaplain about their families because that is *how* we talk about God. That is *how* we talk about the meaning of our lives. That is *how* we talk about the big spiritual questions of human existence.
. . . I have seen such expressions of love: A husband gently washing his wife's face with a cool washcloth, cupping the back of her bald head in his hand to get to the nape of her neck, because she is too weak to lift it from the pillow. A daughter spooning pudding into the mouth of her mother, a woman who has not recognized her for years.
A wife arranging the pillow under the head of her husband's no-longer-breathing body as she helps the undertaker lift him onto the waiting stretcher.
. . . Sometimes that love is not only imperfect, it seems to be missing entirely. Monstrous things can happen in families. Too often, more often than I want to believe possible, patients tell me what it feels like when the person you love beats you or rapes you. They tell me what it feels like to know that you are utterly unwanted by your parents. They tell me what it feels like to be the target of someone's rage. They tell me what it feels like to know that you abandoned your children, or that your drinking destroyed your family, or that you failed to care for those who needed you.
Even in these cases, I am amazed at the strength of the human soul. People who did not know love in their families know that they *should* have been loved. They somehow know what was missing, and what they deserved as children and adults.

When the love is imperfect, or a family is destructive, something else can be learned: forgiveness. The spiritual work of being human is learning how to love and how to forgive. - **Kerry Egan**[133] Doctors and ministers must show their human face and human feelings and to be an integral part of the community that suffers, and not simply outsiders sent to redeem it. Our redeemer took on our suffering and *became as we are*. - **Anthony J. Gittins**[134]

Saint Martin of Tours was the Founder and Patron Saint of Hospital Chaplains. A Roman centurion, he was known to bandage the wounds of soldiers injured on the battlefields. Roles of hospital chaplains today can be specific e.g. rehabilitation, cardiac transplants, children, teamwork, permanent disabilities, amputation or disfigurement, surgery, intensive care, palliative care, faith and identity, organ transplant, dementia, out-patients, terminal illness, ethical issues.

Generic chaplaincy in hospitals is religion nonspecific and denominationally neutral. They provide spiritual care to people of any faith. This raises the question as to what assumptions are made about the nature of spiritual care, the significance of religion, ecumenical views, truth claims and religious commitments? Generic spirituality may speak to all people but as Stephen Pattison writes, 'such a sterile, non-located area of concern may have little of value and substance to offer, least of all those who face problems of life and death.'[135] There is nothing generic about health and sickness, well-being and suffering, as each is a uniquely personal experience.

Doctors, nurses, visitors and patients all go with the territory for the minister of care. In the moments of crisis and failure, the hospital chaplain may have a special responsibility to sustain the physician. These occasions may range from affirming the importance of the doctor's calling to wrestling over an ethical dilemma, assisting or comforting doctors in their constant confrontation with old age, disease and death.[136]

---

[133]Kerry Egan, *My Faith: What people talk about before they die*
http://religion.blogs.cnn.com/2012/01/28/my-faith-what-people-talk-about-before-they-die/
[134]Anthony J. Gittins *Reading the Clouds. Mission Spirituality for New Times*, (Strathfield: St Pauls, 1999), 90-91.
[135]Stephen Pattison, *The challenge of Practical Theology. Selected Essays*, (London: Jessica Kingsley Publishers, 2007), 138.
[136]Evans, 'Healing in the Midst of Dying: A Collaborative Approach to End-of-Life Care,' 171.

In her TED talk, Carolyn Jones offers a tribute to nurses who display great pastoral care. She talks about Sister Stephen, who went into the room of a dying patient, leaned over and said, 'I have to go away for the day, but if Jesus calls you, you go. You go straight home to Jesus.' It was the first time she had witnessed that you could show someone you love them completely by letting go. Again when her own mum was dying, Carolyn noted how the nurses brought her comfort and relief from pain, 'They knew to encourage my sister and I to put a pretty nightgown on my mom, long after it mattered to her, but it sure meant a lot to us. And they knew to come and wake me up just in time for my mom's last breath. And then they knew how long to leave me in the room with my mother after she died.'[137]

One needs to consider the kind of care to provide in varying circumstances. A number of suggestions include:

- Make an appointment before going
- Sometimes a phone call in the morning can be more helpful than a visit
- Do not visit if you are sick
- Tell the staff who you are
- If the door to the patient's room is closed, ask if it is OK to enter
- Stand or sit in line with the patient's vision
- Start with a smile
- Be composed
- Be available
- Be alert for stressors
- Be aware of other things going on such as medical treatment, family visits, etc
- Be sensitive to the person's sickness, fragility and emotional vulnerability
- Be sensitive to the need for rest and quiet

---

[137]Carolyn Jones, 'A tribute to nurses' TED Talks. Filmed Nov 2016
https://www.ted.com/talks/carolyn_jones_a_tribute_to_nurses?utm_source=newsletter_weekly_2017-05-14&utm_campaign=newsletter_weekly&utm_medium=email&utm_content=top_left_button

- Sincere, sustained interest in the whole person, not just the 'sick person'
- Be personal, feel free to ask questions
- Listen intently, nod and respect what is being told
- Help the patient to relax
- Speak to every patient present
- Read facial expressions and body language
- Take a gift
- Allow individuals to open the doors to themselves in their own time and at their own pace
- Leave the room if a doctor arrives
- Help the patient and family members talk about their feelings, fears and worries
- Offer practical help
- Be a link to the outside world
- Communicate with teams and other professionals within the medical setting
- Provide accurate information to dispel confusion and ally fears
- Be a person of prayerful presence
- When you want to help someone, ask first if it is all right to help
- Listen 'between the lines', allowing the person to name their feelings of denial, anger, frustration, depression, sadness or guilt, to say more, to cry, or to reflect silently
- Helping the person to move to acceptance and willingness to continue with life
- Family members will need support as they cope with the changes
- Connect with a person's spirituality through a variety of ways: music, familiar prayers or scripture passages, visiting the local parish church
- Visit more than once, at short intervals, so they can trust in your presence

- Seek to provide facilities to enable the family to remain with a sick child
- Share the comfort of God in reassuring words of Scripture
- Celebrate rituals according to the patient's needs and desires
- During recovery, help the person re-establish a sense of control and enjoyment of life
- Don't stay too long (over half an hour) unless asked
- End with words and gestures of encouragement, for example, making the sign of the cross on the person's forehead, a handshake, or a smile

Many carers prefer long-term visits to better develop a rapport with the person. The visits should continue with 'outpatient chaplaincy' and home visits to enable follow-up.

Although caring for the hospitalised can come naturally, for others it is a challenge. Gerald Niklas notes that, unfortunately, a number of students in the chaplaincy program in hospitals adopt the roles of:

- Medical person, by asking and giving medical information
- Social worker, by obtaining information about social security and nursing homes
- Joy boy, by having a strong need to cheer the patient
- Problem-solver, by listening to the patient's problem for a while and then offering a solution
- Super-professional, by hiding behind his/her profession with so much stiffness that the patient has no feel of the person as a human being.[138]

Gerard Hughes tells the story of an experiment on students studying for ministry, who were visiting a hospital. They were told they were to do a memory test. Someone would read them a story in one room. They would then proceed to another room, where they were to repeat the story as word perfectly as possible. The story read to them was the parable of the good Samaritan. In the corridor between rooms there

---

[138] Gerald R. Niklas, *The Making of a Pastoral Person*, (New York: Alba House, 2001), 21.

was a patient lying in pain and crying for help. The patient was ignored by the single-minded students. Gerard Hughes warns us not to be liable to this loveless single-mindedness.[139]

---

[139] Gerard W. Hughes, *Oh God Why?* (Oxford: The Bible Reading Fellowship, 1993), 178.

Reflection

Usually one can endure pain to a certain degree.
It is called the tolerance threshold.
But when it is watching someone else suffer with debilitating pain,
especially loved ones,
It can be more painful to endure.
Sickness is destructive, exhausting, all-consuming
for those ill and those who wait at the bedside.
In our time of 'being patient' may we:
Find God in the confusion
Discover what really matters in life
Become long suffering
Use this time to be the better person we always wanted to be
Appreciate the caring nature of hospital staff
Accept that letting go of having control is not so bad
Allow the space we inhabit during the illness
become our personal place of deep reflection
Become truly present to God in this time where being busy
has ceased.
Maybe when illness stops us in our tracks,
it is a blessing in disguise,
As our defences are let down, time is now ours,
others have to do the business of caring.
It is our 'patient' time, to be still and know God. Amen.

Chapter 12: Care of the dying

I believe that I shall see the goodness of the Lord in the land of the living. Wait for the Lord; be strong, and let your heart take courage; wait for the Lord! - **Psalm 27:13-14**

I die every day. - **1 Corinthians 15:31**

We have begun to realize, I believe, that the enemy all along was not death, but our own unwillingness to incorporate its reality into our consciousness. - **Sandol Stoddard**[140]

For what is it to die but to stand naked in the wind and to melt into the sun? And what is it to cease breathing but to free the breath from its restless tides, that it may rise and expand and seek God unencumbered? Only when you drink from the river of silence shall you indeed sing. And when you have reached the mountain top, then you shall begin to climb. And when the earth shall claim your limbs, then shall you truly dance. - **Khalil Gibran**[141]

When all is said and done, we're really just all walking each other home - **Ram Dass**[142]

From Scripture

In the Gospels we read of a number of events where Jesus meets the grieving and dying. These include the widow at Nain (Luke 7:11-17), the girl restored to life (Matthew 9:18-26, Mark 5:21-43, Luke 8:40-56), death of John the Baptist (Mark 6:14-29), and raising of Lazarus (John 11:1-44). Jesus faced his own anxieties as well. In John's account at the Last Supper, 'Jesus was troubled in spirit' (John 13:21). At Gethsemane (Mount of Olives), Jesus is in anguish (Matthew 26:36-41, Mark 14:33-42, Luke 22:41-44) and he suffered death on the cross (Matthew 27:46, 50; Mark 15:34, 37; Luke 23:46 and John 19:30).

---

[140]Sandol Stoddard, *The Hospice Movement*, (New York: Vintage Books, 1992), 8.
[141]Khalil Gibran, *The Prophet*, (London: Penguin Books, 1998), 90.
[142]Ram Dass, 'The Road Home' http://www.readthespirit.com/explore/the-ram-dass-interview-on-polishing-the-mirror-you-cant-help-but-smile-hes-still-teaching-us/

Focusing on the account of the washing of the feet (John 13:1-38), 'Jesus knew that his hour had come to depart from the world'. An awareness not only of impending death resulting from jealousy and hatred, but knowing it would come about through a betrayal of friendship, a denial of trust, and abandonment of the disciples. He had hoped to build a community of believers, based on love, but now it threatened to collapse around him, leaving him deserted. Yet despite the pain, the sorrow, the impending failure and loss, Jesus continues his way with the disciples, 'he loved them to the end' (John 13:1).

With Judas and Peter present, Jesus still chose 'to wash the disciples' feet' (John 13:5), despite Peter's protests, perhaps hoping that this loving service would change Judas or Peter's minds and hearts. Death would come viciously, but Jesus loved and served till the very end, wanting his relationship with Peter and Judas to survive whatever threatened to separate them.

So Jesus washed the disciples' feet as an enduring act of love – one not to be forgotten so easily. It is an act that can mean so much for the one washing and the one whose feet are washed. To be that person, after a long day, to sit and allow a dear friend to gently massage your tired feet, to scrub them and tenderly bathe them in soapy water and gently dry them in a warm towel. It feels good.

Or to be the one to rub aching feet, massage and clean and dry them, so the person can relax. It is an act of beautiful service, that forgets all troubles, removes all sense of shame, and settles one into a warm and enduring relationship. Jesus knows and treasures this moment of touch, of recognition, of healing, of reconciliation, of humble service, of gentle companionship. For moments like these, he would risk betrayal, denial, abandonment and death. He invites us to such acts of kindness, as only care for others leaves a lasting impression, 'So if I, your Lord and Teacher, have washed your feet, you also ought to wash one another's feet' (John 13:14).

And yet 'Jesus was troubled in spirit' (John 13:21). Hurting and suffering come, despite our best efforts. Death comes, no matter who we are. Yet will it be all conquering? In facing impending death, one yearns to die true to oneself, to leave a legacy, to love and forgive, to stretch out a hand of warmth to dear ones and to assure those left behind how dear they are. Jesus does just this, remaining till the very end with his disciples, sharing a meal, serving them, loving them and offering parting words, 'I give you a new commandment, that you love one another. Just as I have loved you, you also should love one another' (John 13:34). That is true discipleship, to love no matter the cost. Only such love can transform the world.

Then there is the experience in Gethsemane (Mark 14:32-42). All must pass through inner turmoil and struggle before accepting death, not because we are weak, but because life is precious, is gift. Life has freely and generously given memories of relationships, of love. To let go takes enormous courage and trust that all will be well. Jesus is fully aware of his impending death and takes time out, alone, away from the noise. He takes his disciples to Gethsemane. It is the place all who are dying must pass through – a place of struggle, loneliness and fear. Yet also a place to pray, to find strength, to come to an acceptance.

There are situations in life that will cause suffering and challenge deepest held beliefs. Jesus needed to hear his own heart but he also needed others to affirm him against the wave of doubt that was overshadowing him, 'I am deeply grieved, even to death; remain here, and keep awake' (Mark 14:34). In dying, one needs others there, to be with them, to stand by their side, to affirm beliefs that now appear so frail, to be a support in vulnerability, to be on the lookout for us, keeping all harm away, someone there to hold, to love, to just be there in the silence, a presence, a friend, a confidant. The rest is then up to the dying person, who will let go, knowing someone is there till the very last breath.

Yet the disciples fell asleep for, 'The spirit indeed is willing, but the flesh is weak' (Mark 14:38). Good intentions may be there, and genuineness of heart may exist, but when it comes to putting faith into action, all too often we fail miserably. To love is a value we all hope to aspire to, but Jesus knew well our own weaknesses and selfishness, our betrayals and denials, our fears and failures. The lesson for each person is to learn how to listen to the other, to hear their words of grief, to be attentive to their distress and agitation, and be moved by it. We need to put aside our needs, our tiredness, our fears, and be what the other needs of us, pleads from us, asks of us. We need to be disciples who truly care, who can stand strong in times of suffering, who can stay through trials, ready to face death with hope.

We matter to one another and we need each other. We are better for knowing one another, and we can offer what the other cries out for – affirmation, support, dignity, meaning, loyalty and most importantly undying love. Death can be the final chance to become more fully human not only for the one dying but for those at their bedside. Death brings existence into stark reality yet it is an opportunity for one to assist others find a meaningful conclusion.

Belief in Resurrection

Death is a daily process – physiologically, psychologically and spiritually. Stephen Cave argues that any belief in life after death arises from a 'Terror Management Theory'. People develop worldviews in order to help manage the terror of death. The first is to avoid death. Almost every culture in human history has had some myth or legend of an elixir of life or a fountain of youth, including ancient Egypt, Babylon and India. In European history, there was the work of the alchemists, and today this story is told through science.

The second kind of immortality story is resurrection. It accepts that I'm going to have to die but despite that, I can rise up and live again, as Jesus did. This idea is accepted by Christians, Jews and Muslims. We are reinventing for the scientific age, with the idea of cryonics.

The third is spiritual immortality, that we can leave our body behind and live on as a soul. We are reinventing it for the digital age, by uploading your mind, your essence, the real you, and so live on as an avatar in the ether.

The fourth kind of immortality story is legacy, that you can live on through the echo you leave in the world, like the Greek warrior Achilles, who sacrificed his life fighting at Troy so that he might win immortal fame. Some people leave a more tangible, biological legacy such as children, or as part of some greater whole, a nation or family or tribe, their gene pool.[143]

---

[143]Stephen Cave: The 4 stories we tell ourselves about death. TEDxBratislava · Filmed July 2013
https://www.ted.com/talks/stephen_cave_the_4_stories_we_tell_ourselves_about_death/transcript?language=en

However, despite Stephen Cave's arguments, a transcendent view of life enables people to place their lives and suffering in a larger, meaningful context. The human instinct for 'something beyond the grave,' must be heard as a very powerful part of our being.

> Death and life are not simply two events which follow one upon another and are distinct one from the other in human existence. They interpenetrate one another. We are in process of dying all through our lives, and what we call death is the culminating point of an act of dying that extends over the whole span of life. That is why we are constantly undergoing a foretaste of that descent into death which the Lord took upon himself. Do we not sometimes feel an immeasurable distance lay silently between us and the things of this world, dividing us from them? Are we not slowly in process of becoming those who depart? Are we not constantly and ever anew saying goodbye? Is not that which is familiar to us changing to an ever-increasing extent into that which is alien and almost hostile and repellent? Long before the hour in which we close our eyes for the last time we are already being drawn back into the depths of their world. This descent into the poverty of our own being has already commenced, and has been in progress ever since we received our human natures, even though only in an invisible and hidden manner, at the roots of our being. - **Karl Rahner**[144]

Palaeolithic graves around 50,000 BCE reveal food, weapons, ornaments, and tools found in burial sites, suggesting people believed that the dead continued to exist in a way continuous with this life.

Tribal life offers a corporate personality. The death of an individual is identified with the natural process of birth and death observed in nature and celebrated in tribal ritual.

Christian existence finds its meaning in Christ and hope is the conviction of life in the face of death. The cross is a symbol of the paschal mystery, of the conquest of life over death. God raised Christ to life and thereby made him the bringer of life to all:

---

[144] Karl Rahner, *Theological Investigations*, Vol. VII, (London: Herder and Herder, 1971), 149-150.

Listen, I will tell you a mystery! We will not all die, but we will all be changed, in a moment, in the twinkling of an eye, at the last trumpet. For the trumpet will sound, and the dead will be raised imperishable, and we will be changed. For this perishable body must put on imperishability, and this mortal body must put on immortality. When this perishable body puts on imperishability, and this mortal body puts on immortality, then the saying that is written will be fulfilled: 'Death has been swallowed up in victory.' 'Where, O death, is your victory? Where, O death, is your sting?'
- **1 Corinthians 15:51-55**

The process of dying is surrounded with mystery. People have described feeling a spiritual presence at someone's death, as if the person who died were still there. Others tell of loved ones talking to already deceased family members as they neared death, as if dead loved ones had come to assist in the journey. Dietrich Bonhoeffer beautifully writes:

> No one has yet believed in God and the kingdom of God, no one has yet heard about the realm of the resurrected, and not been homesick from that hour, waiting and looking forward joyfully to being released from bodily existence. Whether we are young or old makes no difference. What are twenty or thirty or fifty years in the sight of God? And which of us knows how near he or she may already be to the goal? That life only really begins when it ends here on earth, that all that is here is only the prologue before the curtain goes up - that is for young and old alike to think about. Why are we so afraid when we think about death? ... Death is only dreadful for those who live in dread and fear of it. Death is not wild and terrible, if only we can be still and hold fast to God's Word. Death is not bitter, if we have not become bitter ourselves. Death is grace, the greatest gift of grace that God gives to people who believe in him. Death is mild, death is sweet and gentle; it beckons to us with heavenly power, if only we realize that it is the gateway to our homeland, the tabernacle of joy, the everlasting kingdom of peace. How do we know that dying is so dreadful? Who knows whether, in our

human fear and anguish we are only shivering and shuddering at the most glorious, heavenly, blessed event in the world? Death is hell and night and cold, if it is not transformed by our faith. But that is just what is so marvellous, that we can transform death.[145]

Stages of death

People don't want to die in hospital. They talk about 'tomorrow,' returning home to family, and friends, returning to work and living an everyday life. They want to work hard and die a natural death. To die the way they live. But often there is no choice.

Thea Bowman wrote, 'When I first found out I had cancer, I didn't know what to pray for. I didn't know if I should pray for healing or life or death. Then I found peace in praying for what my folks call 'God's perfect will.' As it evolved, my prayer has become, 'Lord, let me live until I die.' By that I mean I want to live, love, and serve fully until death comes. If that prayer is answered . . . how long really doesn't matter. Whether it's just a few months or a few years is really immaterial.'[146] She was able to reach acceptance but only by passing through doubt and fear.

Five stages of grieving/dying were formulated by Dr Elizabeth Kubler-Ross in her 1969 book, *On Death* and *Dying*. Not all people go through each stage or experience each in succession. Before Kubler-Ross's own death, she said, 'They were never meant to help tuck messy emotions into neat packages. They are responses to loss that many people have, but there is not a typical response to loss, as there is no typical loss.' The stages include:

Shock - the reaction that forms out of a feeling of disbelief, leaving a feeling of being temporarily numb. Shock can last from a few days to a few weeks, depending on the gravity of the loss.

Stage 1: Denial - gives people time until they are ready to tackle with the necessary changes.

---

[145]Eric Metaxas, *Bonhoeffer. Pastor, Martyr, Prophet, Spy. A Righteous gentile vs. the third reich*, (Nashville: Thomas Nelson, 2010), 531.
[146]Thea Bowman http://www.beliefnet.com/columnists/beyondblue/2010/07/let-me-live-until-i-die-an-int.html

Stage 2: Anger - a result of feeling loss of control in one's life.
Stage 3: Bargaining - buying time one hopes to gain control.
Stage 4: Depression - the person experiences sadness but tries to come to terms with the anticipated loss.

Stage 5: Acceptance – when the reality of death is accepted, one becomes ready to die. Elderly generally move to this acceptance largely on their own, while others may need assistance.

In response to the news of impending death, people also may exhibit spiritual distress which include continued sense of despair, searching or restlessness of spirit. Physical signs include:[147]

- Persistent physical pain or other symptoms that do not seem to have a sustained response to drugs or other treatments when this might be anticipated
- Persistent agitation or restlessness despite addressing potential physical causes
- Repeated questioning about the cause or progression of their underlying illness or unrealistic searching for treatments
- Fear of falling asleep and not waking, or waking up in the early hours and unable to settle again to sleep

Emotional signs include:
- Anxiety
- Seeking constant reassurance
- Unresolved or previously unexpressed grief, anger, loss, family dispute or separation
- Anger at oneself and others
- Persistent tearfulness
- Loss of confidence
- Feeling lost and alone
- Apathy or lack of motivation
- Wanting to die

---

[147]Catholic Bishops' Conference of England and Wales, *A Practical Guide to the Spiritual Care of the Dying Person*, (London: Incorporated Catholic Truth Society, 2010), 11.

Questioning occurs and includes:
- Searching for answers
- Questioning the purpose of suffering
- Questions suggesting a sense of injustice e.g. 'what have I done to deserve this?'
- Self-blame or guilt for previous actions
- Seeking resolution for previous actions, or a desire to heal broken relationships

Regrets of those facing death include:
- I wish I had lived a life true to myself, not as others expected of me
- I wish I had been happier more
- I wish I had the courage to express my feelings
- I wish I had stayed in touch with my family and friends

Preparing for death

Ultimately, life is too short but we can choose how we spend our days, the spaces we create, the meaning we make, the relationships we form, the joy we experience. The journey of life matters.

People who are dying often realise what is most important and what is not, and are often more likely to speak honestly, including words such as please, thank you, forgive me, and I love you. This is because people close to death search for comfort, want to be unburdened and desire existential peace.

The people gathered around a dying person reminds them of their meaningful relationships. The days and moments before death should be a time of reconciliation, a time to communicate forgiveness and a release from hurts inflicted in the past. It is a time for listening and being present and placing the loved one in the hands of Christ. So, during the last days before death, pastoral care frequently takes the form of:
- Sitting with a family
- Encouraging physical touch by the family as a profound way to support a dying person
- Moistening parched lips

- Washing and combing a person's hair to restore a sense of their personal dimension
- Bringing coffee for family members
- Keeping patients clean and the space around them tidy
- Putting an arm around a bereaved member
- Providing opportunity for last words and goodbye to loved ones
- Reconciliation
- Acknowledging the deep sorrow over leaving friends and loved ones behind
- As verbal communication lessens, reassuring family that silence does not mean rejection
- Protecting privacy as each family member may want to say goodbye alone
- Gently urging the family to let go and allow their dear one to die
- Crying with them
- Supporting them in touching the body and talking to it
- Prayer brings closure and is an invitation to separate themselves from the place of death

According to Christopher Swift, the use of ritual acts presents the possibility of meaning in eternal peace, love and happiness. Death can become in certain instances a kind of immanent transcendence.[148]

Palliative/Hospice care

There comes a time when doctors, families and patients need to forgo medical treatment and advances of modern medicine intended to cure or prolong life, and turn to treatment that promotes comfort and preparation for death.

One in four people receives excessive or unwanted medical treatment, or watches a family member receive excessive or unwanted medical treatment. However, Lucy Kalanithi explains that patients have a choice:[149]

---

[148]Christopher Swift, *Hospital Chaplaincy in the Twenty-first Century*, (England: Ashgate, 2009), 133.
[149]Lucy Kalanithi: What makes life worth living in the face of death | TED Talk | TED.com https://www.ted.com/talks/lucy_kalanithi_what_makes_life_worth_living_in_the_face_of_death/transcript?language=en#t-557735

- Would you want to be on life support if it offered any chance of longer life?
- Are you most worried about the quality of that time, rather than quantity?
- Do you want to do dialysis in a clinic or at home?
- What medical care will help you live the way you want to?

One always has a choice, and it is OK to say no to a treatment that's not right for the person.

The Latin word, *hospice*, means both host and guest. Palliative or hospice care is holistic care, where a team of physicians, nurses, home health aides, social workers, chaplains, bereavement counsellors and volunteers all minister to the physical, emotional and spiritual well-being of the terminally ill person, to provide the best possible quality of life.

Hospice offers the opportunity for one to live and die with dignity, love, care and support, surrounded by family. It gives the terminally ill privacy and some measure of control over the remainder of their lives. Hospice care can be delivered in private homes, nursing homes and on rare occasions hospitals. It also encompasses care for bereaved families and others.

In Singapore, hospices are fitted with water, fish and greenery, which provides tranquillity. B. J. Miller tells of a ritual at the Zen Hospice Project in San Francisco where on the death of a resident, they wheel the body out through the garden, all pause and anyone who wants - residents, family, nurses and volunteers - share a story or song or silence, as they sprinkle the body with flower petals. It is a simple parting image to usher in grief with warmth. Contrast that with the typical experience in the hospital setting - floodlit room lined with tubes and beeping machines and blinking lights that don't stop even when the patient's life has. The cleaning crew swoops in, the body is whisked away, and it all feels as though that person had never really existed. Hospitals are places for acute trauma and treatable illness. They are no place to live and die. Life and health and healthcare is not about a disease-centered but a patient- or human-centered model of care.[150]

---

[150] B J Miller – what really happens at the end of life
https://www.ted.com/talks/bj_miller_what_really_matters_at_the_end_of_life/transcript?language=en

In more recent times, principles for Palliative and End-of-Life Care in Residential Aged Care have been developed collaboratively by Palliative Care Australia, Alzheimer's Australia, COTA Australia, Aged & Community Services Australia, Leading Age Services Australia, Catholic Health Australia and the Aged Care Guild to present a united commitment in recognising the diverse needs of residential aged care consumers, families, carers, aged care staff and service providers in providing palliative and end-of-life care. These eight principles are:[151]

1. Consumers' physical and mental needs at end-of-life are assessed and recognised
2. Consumers, families and carers are involved in end-of-life planning and decision making
3. Consumers receive equitable and timely access to appropriate end-of-life care within aged care facilities
4. End-of-life care is holistic, integrated and delivered by appropriately trained and skilled staff
5. The end-of-life care needs of consumers with dementia or cognitive impairment are understood and met within residential aged care
6. Consumers, families and carers are treated with dignity and respect
7. Consumers have their spiritual, cultural and psychosocial needs respected and fulfilled
8. Families, carers, staff and residents are supported in bereavement

The ethical issue of life support

An issue that may arise in caring for the terminally ill is the possibility of euthanasia or when a patient seeks no longer to continue life. *The Australian Code of Ethical Standards* states:

It is never permissible to end a person's life (whether that decision is made to relieve a patient's suffering by euthanasia, to comply with the wishes of the family, to assist suicide, or to vacate a bed). By euthanasia is meant any action or omission which of itself and by intention causes death with the purpose of eliminating all suffering.

---

[151] Principles for Palliative and End-of-Life Care in Residential Aged Care. 2017
http://melbournecatholic.org.au/Portals/0/PCA018_Guiding%20Principles%20for%20PC%20Aged%20Care_W03.pdf

Examples of euthanasia include administering deliberate overdoses of otherwise appropriate medications, and the unjustified withholding or withdrawing of life sustaining forms of care.[152]

Most wish for their loved one a peaceful and dignified death, yet many worry that their decision to terminate life support might make them instrumental in that death. Many have weighed into the debate about proper care for terminally ill patients. Dee Ryall writes in favour of palliative care:[153]

> Many think palliative care is just pain relief but it's much more. Its focus is preventing and relieving suffering and improving quality of life, not just pain relief.
>
> It includes psychological care and spiritual care. It focuses on the individual's needs and those of their family.
>
> Dying is as much a part of life as birth, but unlike birth, it's not something we do well. We know it's cruel to allow someone to die in pain, yet we haven't applied the resources to make sure that doesn't happen.
>
> What we do know is that with expert palliative care, it's possible. The question is: are we willing?

Netflix's documentary *Extremis* released in 2016 on end-of-life care focused on Dr Jessica Zitter, a palliative care specialist and the patients and families, highlighting the tension of end-of-life care: doctors are often able to see the stark reality of a situation before the patients and family can. 'I'm always looking for another miracle', a family member says, and agreeing to pull her mother's tube 'feels like murder'. Difficult questions raised include who ought to make the decisions of when it's time to stop treatment: Can a patient who is severely ill make a clear decision about when and if to withdraw care? At what point should family members take over decision-making from a patient? What is the role of a person's faith even when science seems irrefutable? Even when there is no hope, the idea to make sure all experts and possibilities are considered before giving up, is a need for family members who have promised their dying ones they will do all

---

[152]Code of Ethical Standards, 5.20.
[153]Dee Ryall, 'We have the power to make death dignified with palliative care,' Herald Sun, July 30, 2017
http://www.heraldsun.com.au/news/opinion/we-have-the-power-to-make-death-dignified-with-palliative-care/news-story/13ea296d3c894057d05bf3489a749a37

they can to help them. Other family members see it as God's will and prefer their dying ones to die a natural death. Patients' and families' convictions that this may not be the end are driven by faith or love or belief in medicine. In all cases, there is a reluctance to let go.

Only recently, Dr Stephen Parnis wrote an excellent article in *The Australian*, stating that it's about caring for the most vulnerable and not about supporting assisted suicide:[154]

> The relationship between patient and doctor is based on trust. Patients trust that I will always use my expertise in their best interests. Legalising assisted suicide will fundamentally — and forevermore — breach that trust.
>
> I, and many of my colleagues, cannot accept that the best interests of the patient are ever served by offering them a way to kill themselves.
>
> In an ageing community, we potentially have millions who are vulnerable, who are fearful of becoming a burden, whose suffering is not just physical pain but also isolation or depression. Surely, as a community, we should ask how we can alleviate that suffering, how we can address our society's widespread anxiety about death and dying, how to make quality palliative care truly accessible to all, before reaching for the convenient alternative of an assisted exit.

Through her own experience of facing death, Julie Morgan writes:

> The NSW community is about to debate physician-assisted death or voluntary euthanasia. No doubt one of the key ideas will be the notion that we ought to have a 'free choice' when it comes to the manner of our death. This is coupled with the different understandings that people have about what it means to die with dignity. These are vitally important conversations. However, it often feels to me that the voices who want physician-assisted dying are given extra amplification by celebrities, and that, because they talk about dying with dignity, they somehow must be right. But the past four years have confirmed for me

---

[154] Dr Stephen Parnis, 'Palliative care the answer,' in *The Australian* July 26th 2017
http://www.theaustralian.com.au/opinion/palliative-care-system-being-starved-of-oxygen/news-story/ca1b4c9b006a3e22e994161d98662ee5

everything that my two ethics degrees have taught me: that human dignity is so inherent that it is expressed even in extreme vulnerability and not just in the good times.[155] Patients and families have the right to express their views based on their religious, cultural or familial influence. This matters and determines the choices one makes in regards to prolonging life or terminating.

Discontinuing life support is not euthanasia because it does not introduce a new cause of death, according to ethicists. Morally speaking, the intention is not to cause death but to ease the physical or psychological burden on either the patient or the patient's family. Medical professionals use four criteria to determine the legitimacy of discontinuing mechanical life support:

1. The presence of a fatal condition - If the patient stands a good chance of recovery, life support should by all means be used.
2. The autonomy of the patient - If the patient is conscious, able to communicate, and capable of rational decision making, their desires are paramount. They have every right to refuse a particular medical treatment.
3. Whether the therapy is effective - Doctors may withhold or discontinue treatments that are deemed to be futile, i.e. the patient suffers a terminal condition, the condition is irreversible, and that death is imminent.
4. If a given medical treatment places an excessive burden on the patient, family or community.[156]

From a religious perspective, Christians are expected to use all ordinary means to care for the sick and suffering, such as appropriate feeding, hydration, treatment of infection, comfort, care and hygiene. The Catholic Church permits patients and their families to forgo *extraordinary* care such as discontinuing medical procedures that are burdensome, dangerous, extraordinary, or disproportionate to the expected outcome. It is the refusal of 'over-zealous' treatment. The

---

[155]Julie Morgan 'I'm terminally ill and the debate on euthanasia scares me.' http://www.smh.com.au/comment/im-terminally-ill-and-the-debate-on-euthanasia-scares-me-20170117-gtt0kn.html
[156]Noreen Herzfeld, *Technology and Religion. Remaining human in a co-created world*, (West Conshohocken, PA: Templeton Press, 2009), 50-52.

permanent need for life sustaining machinery, such as a ventilator or dialysis, in the face of terminal illness, is considered extraordinary. It allows for the withdrawal of tube feeding if it is futile or if the patient is experiencing physical suffering or is in a permanently vegetative state (PVS).[157]

---

[157] Herzfeld, *Technology and Religion. Remaining human in a co-created world*, 52.

Reflection

Death.
Unavoidable.
It is dark.
Another world away.
And you must enter alone, releasing your grip on others,
on the world, on life.
The final destiny.
The last journey.
That faltering breath.
It would be wonderfully mysterious
– if one could get over the fear of the unknown.

Others can lead the dying to that door,
Can hold their hand as they take those final steps,
before they're on their own.
Others, family or friends, anyone who cares,
Can be that person at their side,
That presence that holds them up,
Walks with them in darkness,
A voice that offers courage and speaks kind words.

Knowing one is facing death,
And a God they never really knew,
The carer can prepare the dying by speaking words of love
and affirmation.
To hear and know:
Yes, you are good.
Yes, you were made in God's image.
Yes, you are worthy.
Yes, you are forgiven.
And as they pass through life, they may just release their grip
as they hear the words,
'Yes, you are dearly loved.'
They know peace can finally be theirs,
because somebody cared to tell them. Amen.

Chapter 13: Care of the grieving

> Then he began to speak, and taught them, saying . . . 'Blessed are those who mourn, for they will be comforted.'
> **- Matthew 5:4 Beatitudes**
> He will wipe every tear from their eyes. Death will be no more; mourning and crying and pain will be no more, for the first things have passed away.' - **Revelation 21:4**
> But I find myself wondering why I was so contained each time, why so polite. I should have let loose. I should have shrieked and wailed and torn my hair and rent covered myself in ashes. Instead I sat tight, with a hanky dabbed here, an emotion stifled there. I bottled up hot tears like jam, and firmly screwed down the lid. But they won't be stopped. Instead, they come later, inconveniently, in the supermarket, on a crowded tram, when three generations of women sit next to you in a coffee shop, when a bird drops down between two buildings or a certain slant of light stabs you in the eye, when you see a loved one walking and realise it's a stranger and your loved one is dead, when you're washing the dishes and you glance down and the hands in the sink are theirs, when you're cycling at night all alone, all alone; then grief roars up and hits you like a tidal wave . . . Four weeks, three months, ten years later. It doesn't matter how long it's been. Sooner or later, a thousand times over, you're gonna sob. - **Alison Sampson**[158]

Grief in the Gospels

In the Gospels, we read of a number of events where Jesus meets the grieving: the two disciples walking to Emmaus (Luke 24:13-35), the disciples in the upper room (Matthew 28:1-10, Luke 24:36-49, John 20:19-23), Mary Magdalene (John 20:11-18), Thomas (John 20:24-29), Peter (John 21:15-19) and the Beloved Disciple (John 21:20-25).

---

[158] Alison Sampson, *The inevitability of tears*, Eureka Street 2/11/2010
http://www.eurekastreet.com.au/article.aspx?aeid=23722

After Jesus' death, we read how the disciples remain hidden in the upper room, disenchanted with life. Or, as the women do, they head towards the tomb, yearning for the departed to re-enter their lives. Or, as the case with Thomas, who cannot fathom the loss, refuses to accept the way things are. Then there are the seven disciples who go out fishing, perhaps to get away from it all, throwing themselves at their work and repressing their emotions. Underlying all these grieving behaviours, there is the clear message that one is not alone. Jesus is there all along, calling and inviting one to recognise that life goes on and hope remains.

Taking a closer look at the story of Thomas (John 20:24-29), we note that those grieving often seek solitude and lose interest in life. Their fears are heightened and they become less sure of their place in the world. The Gospel reflects these traits as we read, 'A week later his disciples were again in the house, and . . . the doors were shut' (John 20:26). The disciples grieve by huddling together, closing themselves off from the rest of the world. They have become withdrawn. It takes time for one grieving to venture forth again, to find their feet in a world where they have changed and the world has changed. Things are no longer the same for them.

When Jesus appears, he encourages Thomas to touch him. In grief, there is an overwhelming desire to see the person again, to be with them, to touch their flesh, smell their body, hear their voice, and hold them tight. And once the grieved person can feel the presence of a departed one, they find new hope, as Thomas cried out, 'My Lord and my God!' (John 20:28).

Jesus wants to coax the disciples back to life. He comes to pull them out of the grief they are drowning in, to open the doors, to nudge them out of their staleness. The Risen Jesus invites each of us in our losses and grief, to the realisation that there is much more to life and that eternal joy is ours.

In the Emmaus story (Luke 24:13-35), two disciples are travelling on the road, probably to get away from the gloom and to clear their heads over the tragic events that have occurred. When Jesus appears, 'their eyes were kept from recognising him' (Luke 24:16). They were not yet ready to see a new perspective, to experience a new hope. Their grief had blinded them. They say to Jesus as he walks with them, 'Are you the only stranger in Jerusalem who does not know the things that have taken place there in these days?' (Luke 24:18). For these two disciples, the story of their grief is all encompassing, so much so that it looms large in their minds and overshadows everything else. Their conversation revolves around the one who has died. It is in their minds, their words, day and night, consuming them. Grief needs to relive over and over again the story of the one who has died, for fear that they may be forgotten.

Jesus travels with the two disciples, sharing their story, but also inviting them to see it from another perceptive. He offers them new insight, gives meaning to what seems futile, and honours their journey as he moves them from sorrow to a new stage in life.

The two disciples invite Jesus to spend the night with them, for grieving people need company and support. Jesus accepts, willing to be there for those who call out, and in those moments of gentle understanding and companionship, those who dwell in darkness, come to see a new dawning.

We can also better understand grieving by reflecting over the story when the disciples go fishing (John 21:1-14). Slowly the call to resume life begins to be heard. Simon Peter goes fishing accompanied by six other disciples. They probably needed to fish in order to eat, but how much of an appetite does a grieving person have? Going fishing was probably a way to get out onto the lake, to be left alone, to have the time to ponder over past events.

The fishing expedition is unsuccessful as we read, 'that night they caught nothing' (John 21:3). Perhaps they just wanted to sit in that boat, in the dark, on the lake, away from reality. They remain at a distance, until daybreak. Then Jesus appears.

When instructed by Jesus to cast the net one more time, the haul of fish is significant. Suddenly the disciples are wakened from their stupor. Jesus has jolted them back into the world where there is fish to be caught, work to be done, mouths to feed and it is business as usual. The distaste for life that accompanies grief, sooner or later, is left behind for the demands of everyday life.

Jesus reminds the disciples of the joy of a good catch, the pleasure of sharing a meal as he prepares them breakfast, and the memories that are made as one gathers with good company. Jesus returns after death to remind us that life is worth living abundantly, even after grief.

Funerals

According to Stephen R. Covey, we must ask ourselves what is the meaning of my life? He offers an exercise: to sit down, collect your thoughts and focus. Think of three people you know well:
- Family member
- Friend
- Work colleague

Now imagine yourself sitting at the back of a long church while everyone you know is sitting in front of you. Suddenly, you realise you are watching your own funeral, years from now. The three people you have chosen will be doing your obituary. What would you like each one to say about you and your life? How do you want them to remember you? Write it all down. One may be surprised as to what emerges on paper. It may clarify what one's deepest desires are. It is an exercise that carers can do to better understand those facing death and grief.

In early times, Christian funerals involved visitation at home, where the family washed, dressed and sat with the body in recognition that it was sacred. The visitation was traditionally a period of waiting with the body until the procession stopped for a service at the church, then continued on to accompany the deceased until they were laid to rest. The grave was probably in the churchyard near other deceased relatives. Mourners could continue to visit and remember the dead, who remained part of the church community.[159] A visit to graves can be one of the most meaningful and important pilgrimages one makes as they let go of a loved one.

Today, the Christian funeral continues to give shape to grief as the community expresses its faith and ties the emotions following death into the larger story of humanity's fall into sin, redemption and the re-creation of the world. People come to the funeral with raw emotions,

---
[159] Rob Moll, *The Art of Dying* (Downers Grove, Illinois: IVP Books, 2010), 120.

feelings of guilt. If guilt and anger are to be understood and forgiven, only the language of liturgy and prayer will do, notes Alan Billings. In the absence of the deceased, only God can forgive. In the funeral service, there is a form of confession and absolution, prayers of forgiveness, as well as a time for private prayer.[160]

The service honours the loved one and allows the bereaved to publicly express that person's significance in their lives and the life of the community. Death becomes a private affair but also a social one. As Jeffrey Essmann writes:[161]

> My niece was buried a few weeks ago, a wonderful young woman: 36, not sick, suddenly gone. Sudden deaths, they say, are the most traumatic — and certainly sudden deaths of the young. The shock is nearly concussive.
>
> Just before Mass started, I looked around the room at a church filled with people who loved my niece and thought, this is who she really was, is: this texture of relationships, these people with whom she experienced connection and love, who now, for her sake, for love of her, comfort one another, hold one another, cry. And at the Our Father, as I stood hand-in-hand praying with my sister and her family, I suddenly felt everything beneath the text and the ritual shift, everything slip and move into that pure, primal place a funeral conjures, where we are a stone-age clan burying a kinsman at the back of the cave; where we are the builders of pyramids, temple mourners, necromancers; where we are the heartbroken friends of a crucified man getting him to a tomb before the Sabbath.
>
> We are all of us in pain, all stunned at the sudden emptiness, all plunged into the mystery at the heart of sadness, all awestruck at the strange life that pulses faintly within the fog of loss. We have all of us been brought to holy ground, thrown to it, dazed, all of us brought to a place beyond words.

---

[160] Alan Billings, *Secular Lives, Sacred Hearts: The Role of the Church in a Time of No Religion*, (London: SPCK, 2004), 91-99.
[161] Jeffrey Essmann, Grappling with the meaning of sadness. 11 March 2016 http://cathnews.com/cn-perspectives/24517-the-mystery-of-sadness

The church maintains a constant presence from illness, to dying, to the burial and to the grieving. There is an affirmation of the human body, and a commemoration of the person and the life they lived. Singing hymns, reading Scripture and hearing God's word preached is how the church displays its hope. The funeral rite understands that those passed away can be reached by the prayer of the faithful. Belief in the resurrection is represented by a headstone with a cross, and a powerful message of concreteness of that particular person, with their name and the date on the headstone. Amy Plantinga Pauw writes, 'The church will gather to celebrate our life and mourn our passing, and confident that the community will care for our family through prayers, visits, and generous hospitality.'[162] People pray closely to the dead body, support the bereaved family and live the funeral Eucharist.

Stages of Grief

Bereavement is the loss of someone or something vital to one's life. With the death of a loved one there is a loss of meaning and a connection with the past. It leaves an inner emptiness, disorientation, confusion and anguish. Grief is acknowledging the pain of loss. To cope with bereavement of death, one needs to welcome all the little bereavements which begin early on in life. It cannot be overcome simply by logic or rational discussion and it is not about 'getting over' the loss of a significant other. It is about finding new ways to be spiritually connected, and reconstructing stories and practices that represent who the griever and the grieved are.

Steven L. Jeffers and Harold Ivan Smith detail the numerous models of grieving that have been suggested. Included in the list is Colin Murray Parkes' *Bereavement – A study of grief in adult life*, five stages of grieving.[163]

1. Alarm/Shock/Numbness – Can occur in the first 2 weeks after death or on special occasions. The finality of the actual death is disturbing at a deep level for survivors. Protesting loss occurs through avoidance or denial. Often sleep disturbance and

---

[162] Amy Plantinga Pauw, 'Dying well' in *Living well and dying Faithfully*, John Swinton and Richard Payne (ed.), (Grand Rapids, Michigan: William B. Eerdmans Publishing Company, 2009), 20.
[163] Steven L. Jeffers and Harold Ivan Smith, *Finding a sacred oasis in grief. A resource manual for pastoral caregivers*, (Oxford: Radcliffe Publishing, 2007).

disorientation occurs. The body needs time to process the changes. Allow the bereaved to reminisce about the past. It allows them to redefine their relationship with the deceased.

2. Searching – Can be 4-6 weeks after death but is on and off over the years. It is a time of pining and intense yearning for the dead person, continuing to act as if the person were alive. They find themselves alone and aware that death has occurred. Feelings of anger, powerlessness, anxiety, guilt or helplessness. Recalling their loved one is necessary.

3. Mitigation – Occurs around the third or fourth month. It includes depression and deep despair. The emptiness is painful and difficult. Presence changes to memory. Friends need to be there to listen and support.

4. Anger/Guilt – Emotional turmoil in the fifth and sixth months.

5. Identity/Recovery – About six months later, they are better able to cope and can re-join past activities. Eventually, new patterns are formed, new relationships developed and new identity emerge. It is readjusting to the loss.

There are many other theories of grief.[164] Howard Clinebell explains that the movement from the initial shock of loss to the ultimate experience of new life involves tasks with which the companionship of a caregiver can be helpful:[165]

---

[164]Steven L. Jeffers and Harold Ivan Smith, *Finding a sacred oasis in grief. A resource manual for pastoral caregivers*, (Oxford: Radcliffe Publishing, 2007), 85-86, 90-91. Therese Rando produced a model called the 6 R Processes of Mourning (*Treatment of Complicated Mourning* 1993, p45). 1. Recognise the loss 2. React to the separation. 3. Recollect and re-experience the deceased and the relationship. 4. Relinquish the old attachments to the deceased 5. Readjust to move adaptively into the new world without forgetting the old 6. Reinvest. Wayne Oates suggests grief is expressed in six stages: 1. Shocking blow of loss-in-itself 2. Numbing effect of the shock 3. Struggle between fantasy and reality 4. Break-through of a flood of grief 5. Selective memory and stabbing pain. 6. And acceptance of loss and reaffirmation of life itself. David Switzer recognises four common phases of grief: 1. Feeling of numbness and denial 2. Yearning for and preoccupation with thoughts of the deceased person 3. Disorganisation and despair. 4. Reorganization of behaviour. William Worden defines the grief process in terms of tasks to be accomplished. 1. To accept reality of loss. 2. To work through the pain of grief. 3. To adjust to an environment in which the deceased is missing. 4. To emotionally relocate and memorialise the deceased.

[165]Howard Clinebell, *Basic Types of Pastoral Care & Counseling: Resources for the Ministry of Healing and Growth*, (Abingdon Press, 2012), 190-195.

Task one: Dealing with numbness and shock – Severe losses activate the griever's 'inner child', often bringing painful feelings of anxiety, deprivation, and abandonment. Effective caring includes using supportive care methods which gratify dependency needs.

- Task two: Expressing and talking through feelings as they are gradually released – one primary goal of grief work is to make the relationships that have been lost in external reality strongly and vividly internal in survivors' minds and hearts. Repetitive reminiscing and storytelling help them accomplish this. The key feelings that most often infect the grief wounds are unresolved guilt, anger and fear.
- Tasks three and four: Coping and then rebuilding – caregivers should encourage persons weathering crises and grief to be kind and gentle with themselves and to let those in the circle of mutual care know that they need extra support and loving.
- Task five: Enhancing spiritual and ethical wholeness – the symbols and affirmations of one's religious tradition can touch deep levels of the psyche, gradually renewing the feelings of basic trust in life that can enable persons to handle existential anxiety creatively.
- Task six: Reaching out for mutual support and care.

In a time of loss and bereavement, when basic questions of life and meaning are challenged, religious and spiritual influences can be critical. Looking at Jesus' death and resurrection, there are five distinct moments within the paschal cycle, as Ronald Rolheiser suggests:[166]

1. Good Friday – the loss of life, real death
2. Easter Sunday – the reception of new life
3. The Forty Days – a time for readjustment to the new and for grieving the old
4. Ascension – letting go of the old and letting it bless you, the refusal to cling
5. Pentecost – the reception of new spirit for the new life that one is already living

---

[166]Ronald Rolheiser, *The Holy Longing. The Search for a Christian Spirituality*, (New York: Doubleday, 1999), 147.

Each is part of the process of transformation, of dying and letting go, so as to receive new life and new spirit. This cycle is something undergone daily, in every aspect of one's life. Christ spoke of daily deaths, many risings and various Pentecosts. After death, loss, rejection and failure, life does go on.

Gerard Hughes uses the Scripture in a way to allow the person to express their grief. He suggests - for those who are afflicted with gloom - to pray and imaginatively contemplate the raising of Lazarus in John 11.

Have a good look at Lazarus in his tomb. He is dead, corrupting, enclosed in darkness. Then hear the voice outside the tomb saying: 'I am the resurrection. If anyone believes in me, even though he dies he will live, and whoever lives and believes in me will never die.' Without forcing anything, let your own feelings of sadness and depression surface in your consciousness so that you see yourself locked within the tomb of your own sadness. Then hear the stone being removed and hear the voice of Jesus calling you by name, '... arise, come forth.'

Sometimes, people who pray in this way discover that they do not want to emerge from the tomb. This is not failure, but an important discovery, showing them that they are in the tomb of sadness not because God wills them to be there, but because they have chosen to be there. If this were to happen to you, do not be alarmed, but acknowledge your attachment to the tomb and keep asking Christ to set you free.[167]

Children

Even though death of a loved one may have been anticipated for months, the finality of their loss sinks in only after the funeral and burial have taken place. This is the time when a family comes to terms with their relationships with the deceased and start to readjust their lives and home.

Mothers who miscarry early in pregnancy may experience the same intensity of grief as those who carry the baby full term resulting in a stillbirth. Parents lose their dreams and hopes for the child, lose part

---

[167] Gerard W. Hughes, *God of Surprises*, (London: Darton, Longman and Todd Ltd, 2003), 138-139

of themselves and a part of each other, possibilities of parenthood and they lose their future. What parents need is for family, friends and loved ones to acknowledge their loss.[168] Naming, blessing, memorialising or simply touching and holding the baby are rituals to help say goodbye. Family members will also grieve as the baby is someone's granddaughter, brother, cousin, nephew or sister.

In caring for grieving children 6 years and under, adults must be clear on what they are saying and what is being heard. A child over the age of six is developmentally tackling the concept of life and death. They do not comprehend the finality of death. Yet when we tell them that someone they love has died, they accept that something has happened. Their pain is in their separation.[169]

Children's grief has many dimensions including:

- Apparent lack of feelings - more likely to be emotional shock and a protective mechanism.

- Regression - may occur during stressful times. They may wish to be held and rocked or ask a parent to do their shoe lace, because they fear separation from them.

- Big man syndrome – in order to replace the person who is gone, children may begin to express adult behaviour before their time.

- Acting out – they express their hurt through anger, resentment and blame. These are explosive emotions behind pain, helplessness, frustration and fear.

- Loss and loneliness – expressed through lack of interest in themselves, change in appetite or sleeping patterns, nervousness, inability to enjoy life and low self-esteem.

- Feel as if 'something' has been ripped from them - children are more susceptible to this sense of betrayal particularly if the deceased is a parent or close loved one.

- Reconciliation – children return to stable eating and sleeping patterns and a renewed sense of well-being, although grief may stop by briefly during birthdays and holidays.[170]

---

[168]Steven L. Jeffers and Harold Ivan Smith, *Finding a sacred oasis in grief. A resource manual for pastoral caregivers*, (Oxford: Radcliffe Publishing, 2007), 41, 45-46.
[169]John Spivey and Shelly Hartwick, 'Grief and Bereavement' in *Hospice, a labor of love*, (St. Louis, Missouri: Chalice Press: 1999), 82-83.
[170]Spivey and Hartwick, 'Grief and Bereavement,' 83-85.

Teenagers and Adults

Feelings and symptoms that grieving teenagers and adults experience at the death of a loved one include:
- Identity crisis and corresponding loss of self-worth
- Question the purpose of life
- Bouts of depression and sadness
- Guilty or pessimistic
- Irritability and excessive anger
- Confrontational
- Accident proneness or forgetfulness
- Thoughts are unfocused, repetitive and preoccupied
- Difficulty making decisions
- Less talkative or uneasy and restless
- Significant changes in personal appearance, facial expression and eye contact, eating habits, changes in personal norms and interests
- Change in sleeping patterns and headaches
- Feelings of restlessness and looking for activity
- Having low energy or lethargy
- Regressing to immature behaviours, clinging behaviours, social withdrawal or avoidance
- Tightness in the throat and heaviness in the chest
- Sighing and an empty feeling in the stomach
- Stealing, promiscuity and illegal behaviour such as smoke, alcohol or use of drugs

The event requiring the greatest amount of social readjustment is the death of a spouse. Sharp feelings of anger, intense sadness, abandonment, loss of trust, guilt, helplessness, resentment, suicidal thoughts, feelings of revenge, can all be present at different times. Other signs of one grappling with loss of a dear one include:
- Need to tell and retell the story of the loved one's death
- Intensely angry at loved one for 'being left'

- Crying at unexpected times
- Sensing and hearing the loved one
- Expecting the loved one to come home any minute
- Assuming mannerisms or traits of the loved one
- Yearning to be with the loved one or see them again

Ways caregivers can provide pastoral care in the phase of grief include:

- Be present as soon as possible when you hear about a death
- Let your genuine concern and care show
- Provide a safe place for them to express their grief, share their loss
- Be open about the pain, anguish, anger or even revolt
- Assure them that their grief counts
- Allow the grieving to speak of death, to talk about the person who has left
- Help families unburden themselves through listening to their reassessment of their decisions and by reaffirming the integrity of their choices
- Respond understandingly - and without judgment - to feelings stated strongly
- An empathic statement such as, 'It must be very difficult for you' gives the bereaved permission to make an active response
- Take over some things temporarily, managing them for the bereaved, then passing the responsibility back when they are ready
- Talk about the person who has died as it is a relief to them to know that someone will use their name and remembers something about them
- Give expression to hope
- Help find religious/spiritual practices that connect them with God and a sense of the sacred

People often remember less about the content of words than they do about the way one treated them - with gentleness, respect, graciousness and sensitivity.

Grieving Elderly

One simple way to help elders who grieve is for the carer to visit them at home or call them on the telephone. It reassures them that they are still part of the community. A church can form a visitors team through volunteers in the congregation who can:
- Visit
- Listen to them and validate their feelings
- Let them talk about their health problems, death of loved ones, changes in their lives, etc.
- Gently encourage them to visit or phone others
- Encourage the elderly to overcome their loneliness by helping someone in need.

Time and grace will change and heal the grieving. Life will interrupt, the phone will ring, emails will fill inboxes, laughter will rise unexpectedly, friends will visit, tears will cleanse and family demands won't cease. Joyce Rupp captures the idea that life will go on:[171]

> I sat on the doorstep of my porch, talking on the phone, listening to a newly widowed friend speak of her severe sorrow. In between wrenching tears, she poured out her struggle of attempting to re-engage with a life that no longer included her beloved husband. As I gave full attention to my grieving friend, a young, sleek deer emerged from the woods and stood like a sentinel on the front lawn. At the same time, the tiny lights of fireflies began twinkling in the night air. I felt caught between two contrasting worlds: the sharp pain in my friend's heart and the alluring beauty of the natural world. Between these two opposites, something unidentified nudged me to pay attention. I let the disparity be there until the phone conversation ended. Then I continued to sit silently on the doorstep, pondering the enticing scene, wondering what stirred inside of me. This movement opened the door to my inner self and led me to look at that part that always wants to be fair. I recognised my strong desire to relieve my friend of her heartache. At that same time, I

---

[171] Joyce Rupp, *Open the door. A journey to the truth self,* (Notre Dame, Indiana: Sorin Books, 2008), 16-17.

also trusted she was in a 'growing place' and eventually would be less pained from her loss. From this pause of reflection, I glimpsed divine presence in both areas: a Compassionate Companion embracing hurting ones and a Generous Creator continually revealing abundant splendour. The deer and the fireflies assured me that beauty remains present in the midst of life's turmoil. That evening the door of my heart proved a passageway to gratitude for enduring beauty and a reminder to trust God's strength to be there, especially when the harshness of life shows its face.

A carer helps people transition through grief as fellow sojourners on earth. There are no simple answers, no formulas, or rituals. Ultimately, one stands with the bereaved, along with God, to help them through a difficult time.

Reflection

When you died, Jesus,
That day between your burial and your resurrection
That Easter Saturday, that empty day
Life still went on for people
But for us who have known you,
On that day life stopped.
No meaning anymore, nothing to live for.
But we cry, 'God cannot be dead. God can't be forgotten'.
You are much bigger than life
Much more important.
And so you burst onto the scene again because
Without you, life doesn't really function.
You live God, and because of you, we live.

When our loved ones pass on,
Our dear, dear ones,
There is emptiness, a dull numbing.
We pine for them
But they will no longer return to us, as they were.
We miss them, yearn for them, need them.
But they are gone.
Gone, we pray, into your loving presence,
O God, greater than life.
Gather them into your arms
Just as a mother hen gathers her brood
under the safety of her wings.
Take our dearly beloved ones, God,
And embrace them with your gentle compassion.
Love them for us, care for them
As your own dear children.

As for us who dwell on this earth,
Yearning for the time to be united with you and our loved ones,
Embrace us,

Let us find warmth and comfort
Knowing you eternally care, O God of life.
We need you now.
We rest in your tender presence.
Grant us your strength and peace
To go on with life. Amen.

Conclusion

To care may not be a popular term in today's society where attributes such as self-starter, beauty, intelligence, humour and physical strength garner a huge following. However, to be one that cares is a result of cultivating many attributes into a character that can overstep personal wants to act on behalf of a greater good.

Power without morality is ruthless, beauty without heart is cold, and knowledge without action is dead. Whatever we do will be measured by its outcome, its influence on others and its contribution to society. If care is practised, it releases possibilities, encourages the best in others, binds people in love, heals division, and permits hope to transform lives.

To care is to make the other matter, to use one's personal resources in order to help. It is to respond appropriately in circumstances, making qualities of love, compassion and healing, a power for good. In caring, one exhibits a depth of understanding and a response that profoundly affects others.

Jesus' impression was lasting for the quality of care he showed time and time again. What touches hearts and frees minds and offers genuine love, will endure. So what will we be remembered for? What legacy will we leave behind? Do we want to care? For surely every single person, no matter what other qualities or attributes they have or don't have, each person has been gifted with the capability of caring. Nothing else is more important or needed than the ability to care and thus create a world where good abounds over hurt, hate and harm.

Pastoral care - or call it spiritual concern or just simply caring - is nothing new but has been an action, an attitude and a virtue from time immemorial and withstands fads, popularity and trends. It cannot be abandoned and there will come a time where each person will need care or will show care. It constitutes what it is to be human. To refuse to care, to withhold care, to deny care, or to hinder care, is to allow apathy to claim victory.

Caring thus becomes a necessity. It is tied closely with compassion and mercy and extends from empathy to justice, from love to advocacy, from personal commitment to community engagement. It transforms the hearts and lives of all involved and is what heals each one of us, once the storm of pain and turmoil subsides.

How do we care? It starts from the heart. When it is attracted by others, it wants to give. It starts simply, with a smile that is so contagiously disarming, with a touch that can be ever so soft and yet emotionally recharges another, and with a gentle word that unknowingly can lift the spirit. A listening ear, a look of love, an attentive presence, are all ways that offer dignity and support.

Yet pastoral care isn't just a feel good emotion. It picks up the fragments of life shattered by experiences, and pieces them slowly and thoughtfully together. Through care, one experiences the brokenness and sorrow in the world, but comes armed with another experience of beauty and hope which is gifted to those who cannot just yet see goodness.

In desiring healing and wholeness, one commits oneself to ever greater offerings of care. Jesus understood this when he proclaimed towards the end of his life, in John's Gospel, 'This is my commandment, that you love one another as I have loved you. No one has greater love than this, to lay down one's life for one's friends' (John 15:12-13). Care becomes a force driven by the heart, motivated by the will, committed through experience, and revolutionary in its actions. It has the vulnerable in its embrace, but wields justice against anything that harms. Care is a force to be reckoned with.

To cultivate an attitude that cares is a work in progress. It is to want to, to choose to be the better person. But that takes time and practice. Surrounded by many things that entice us into a selfish way of living, there must be a deliberate decision to choose otherwise. To want to be better people is to cultivate within one the practice of reflection, inner peace, deeper prayer, immersion in the life of Jesus, desire to seek out and save the lost, to put others before oneself.

Reflection

The deepest human desire,
To be like God.
To dare to offer radical kindness.
To aid those in desperate need.
Not to wait for a reward,
But to freely give a warm, kind word
that is desperately needed but dared not asked for.
To loose sins and release from oppression all that binds.
Ah, if only we could become the miracle of love.

Bibliography

American Psychological Association: What causes a person to have a particular sexual orientation? http://www.apa.org/topics/lgbt/orientation.aspx

Australian Catholic Bishops Conference, *Anointed and Sent. An Australian Vision for Catholic Youth Ministry*, Second Edition, 2014 http://evangelisationbrisbane.org.au/assets/uploads/anointed-and-sent.pdf

Bailey, V., Baker, A-M., Cave, L., Fildes, J., Perrens, B., Plummer, J. and Wearring, A. 2016, *Mission Australia's 2016 Youth Survey Report, Mission Australia*. 2016 https://www.missionaustralia.com.au/publications/research/young-people

Benner, David G. *Care of Souls. Revisioning Christian Nurture and Counsel*. Grand Rapids, Michigan: Baker Books, 1998.

Billings, Alan. *Secular Lives, Sacred Hearts: The Role of the Church in a Time of No Religion*, London: SPCK, 2004.

Brous, Sharon. *It's time to reclaim religion*. TEDWomen 2016 · Filmed October 2016 · 16:27 http://www.ted.com/talks/sharon_brous_it_s_time_to_reclaim_and_reinvent_religion/transcript?language=en

Bowman, Thea. http://www.beliefnet.com/columnists/beyondblue/2010/07/let-me-live-until-i-die-an-int.html

Cassidy, Sheila. *Light from the Dark Valley*. London: Darton, Longman and Todd, 1994.

Catholic Bishops Conference of England and Wales, *A Practical Guide to the Spiritual Care of the Dying Person*, London: Incorporated Catholic Truth Society, 2010. http://www.cbcew.org.uk/CBCEW-Home/About-Us/Documents-and-Publications

Catholic Health Australia. *Code of Ethical Standards for Catholic Health and Aged Care Services in Australia*, 2001.
http://www.stvincents.com.au/assets/files/pdf/CodeofEthicalStandards.pdfC

Cavanagh, Michael E. *The Effective Minister: Psychological and Social Considerations.* San Francisco: Harper and Rowe, 1986.

Cave, Stephen. The 4 stories we tell ourselves about death. TEDxBratislava · Filmed July 2013 · 15:33
https://www.ted.com/talks/stephen_cave_the_4_stories_we_tell_ourselves_about_death/transcript?language=en

Chittister, Joan D. *Two Dogs and a Parrot: What Animals Can Teach Us About the Meaning of Life.* US: BlueBridge, 2015.

Chittister, Joan D. *Heart of Flesh.* Grand Rapids, Michigan: Wm B Eerdmans Pub, 1998.

Chittister, Joan D. *Scarred by Struggle, Transformed by Hope.* Grant Rapids, Michigan: William B. Eerdmans Pub. Co, 2003.

Chittister, John OSB. 'Growing Older Gracefully.' *The Gift of Years* 2008.
http://spirituality.ucanews.com/2014/10/13/growing-older-gracefully/

Clebsch, William A. and Charles R. Jaekle. *Pastoral Care in Historical Perspective.* New York: John Aronson, 1983.

Clinebell, Howard. *Basic Types of Pastoral Care & Counseling: Resources for the Ministry of Healing and Growth.* Abingdon Press, 2012.

Connolly, Noel. *A great welcome for ourselves.*
https://www.columban.org.au/media-and-publications/newsletters-and-bulletins/columban-ebulletin/archive/2016/e-news-vol.9-no.6/fr-noel-connolly-a-great-welcome-for-ourselves?quip_thread=article15410&quip_parent=1123

Dass, Ram. 'The Road Home'
http://www.readthespirit.com/explore/the-ram-dass-interview-on-polishing-the-mirror-you-cant-help-but-smile-hes-still-teaching-us/

Dillard, Annie. *Teaching a stone to talk*. New York: Harper and Row, 1982.

Doehring, Carrie. *The Practice of Pastoral Care: A Postmodern Approach*. Kentucky: Westminster John Knox Press, 2015.

Egan, Kerry. *My Faith: What people talk about before they die* http://religion.blogs.cnn.com/2012/01/28/my-faith-what-people-talk-about-before-they-die/

Essmann, Jeffrey. Grappling with the meaning of sadness. 11 March 2016 http://cathnews.com/cn-perspectives/24517-the-mystery-of-sadness

Evans, Abigail Rian. 'Healing in the Midst of Dying: A Collaborative Approach to End-of-Life Care' in *Living well and dying Faithfully*, John Swinton and Richard Payne (ed.), Grand Rapids, Michigan: William B. Eerdmans Publishing Company, 2009:165-187.

Frankl, Victor. *Man's search for meaning*. Boston: Beacon Press, 2006.

Gadamer, Hans-Georg. *Truth and Method*, trans. by Joel Weisheimer and Donald G. Marshall. Crossroad, 1989.

Gibran, Khalil. *The Prophet*. London: Penguin Books, 1998

Gittins, Anthony J. *Called to Be Sent*. Missouri: Ligouri, 2008.

Gittins, Anthony J. Reading *the Clouds. Mission Spirituality for New Times*, Strathfield: St Pauls, 1999.

Glen, Genevieve, Marilyn Kofler and Kevin O'Connor. *Handbook for Ministers of Care*. Chicago: Liturgy Training Publications, 1997.

Gollnick, James. *Religion and Spirituality in the Life Cycle*, NY: Peter Lang, 2008.

Graham, Elaine L. *Words made flesh. Writings in pastoral and practical Theology*. London: SCM Press, 2009.

Griffin, John Howard. *Prison of Culture: Beyond Black Like Me*. Texas: Wings Press, 2011.

Groome, Thomas H. *What makes us Catholic. Eight gifts for life*. NY: Harper San Francisco, 2002.

Gula, Richard M. *Just Ministry. Professional Ethics for Pastoral Ministers*. New York: Paulist Press, 2010, 130.

Gutierrez, Gustavo. *A Theology of Liberation*. Maryknoll, New York: Orbis, 1973.

Hamilton, Maggie. 'What's happening to our boys and girls?' *At Happiness & Its Causes 2011 Conference*.
https://www.youtube.com/watch?v=6T8QIiU09pc

Headlee, Celeste. TED Talks 10 ways to have a better conversation, Posted Feb 2016
http://www.ted.com/talks/celeste_headlee_10_ways_to_have_a_better_conversation/transcript?language=en

Herzfeld, Noreen. *Technology and Religion. Remaining human in a co-created world*. West Conshohocken, PA: Templeton Press, 2009.

Hughes, Gerard W. *God of Surprises*. London: Darton, Longman and Todd Ltd, 2003.

Hughes, Gerard W. *Oh God Why?* Oxford: The Bible Reading Fellowship, 1993.

Integrity in Ministry. A Document of Principles and Standards for Catholic Clergy & Religious in Australia. Reprinted 2010. Paragraph 1.4
https://www.catholic.org.au/documents/1344-integrity-in-ministry-2010-1/file

Jeffers, Steven L. and Harold Ivan Smith, *Finding a sacred oasis in grief. A resource manual for pastoral caregivers*, Oxford: Radcliffe Publishing, 2007:40-65.

Jones, Carolyn. 'A tribute to nurses' TED Talks. Filmed Nov 2016
https://www.ted.com/talks/carolyn_jones_a_tribute_to_nurses?utm_source=newsletter_weekly_2017-05-14&utm_campaign=newsletter_weekly&utm_medium=email&utm_content=top_left_button

Kalanithi, Lucy. What makes life worth living in the face of death | TED Talk | TED.com
https://www.ted.com/talks/lucy_kalanithi_what_makes_life_worth_living_in_the_face_of_death/transcript?language=en#t-557735

Kaska, Danusia Homelessness has many faces, 19 June 2017
https://www.eurekastreet.com.au/article.aspx?aeid=52594#.WUhRvmiGOU1

Kidd, Robert A. 'Foundational listening and responding skills' in *Professional Spiritual & Pastoral Care: A Practical Clergy and Chaplain's Handbook*, edited by Stephen B. Roberts. SkyLight Paths Publishing, US, 2013.

Lartey, Emmanuel Y. *Pastoral Theology in an Intercultural World*. Ohio: The Pilgrim Press, 2006.

Lee, Elizabeth. 'Prison Ministry has Changed Me.' *Eremos* Sept 2014, No 128. Pages 16-19.

Litchfield, Kate. *Tend my flock. Sustaining good pastoral care*. Norwich: Canterbury Press, 2006.

Loader, Bill. *Ordination charge*
http://wwwstaff.murdoch.edu.au/~loader/charge.html

Loneliness Survey Finds Australians Are Very, Very Lonely – VICE
https://www.vice.com/en_au/article/loneliness-survey-finds-that-australians-are-very-lonely

Lopez, Frank. *Applied Pastoral Care: A Contextual Approach*, Hunters Hill: Marist Centre for Pastoral Care, 1995.

Mari, Jean-Paul. *The chilling aftershock after a brush with death*
http://www.ted.com/talks/jean_paul_mari_the_chilling_aftershock_of_a_brush_with_death/transcript?language=en

McCormick, Phyliss. 'Crabbit Old Woman'
http://mrmom.amaonline.com/stories/CrabbitOldWoman.htm

Merton, Thomas. Speech in Calcutta. *The Asian Journal of Thomas Merton*. 1968.

Metaxas, Eric. *Bonhoeffer. Pastor, Martyr, Prophet, Spy. A righteous gentile vs. the third reich.* Nashville: Thomas Nelson, 2010.

Miller, B. J. What really happens at the end of life https://www.ted.com/talks/bj_miller_what_really_matters_at_the_end_of_life/transcript?language=en

Moll, Rob. *The Art of Dying.* Downers Grove, Illinois: IVP Books, 2010.

Moran, Frances M. *Beyond the culture of care. Helping those souled-out by the market economy.* NSW: St Pauls, 2006.

Morgan, Julie. 'I'm terminally ill and the debate on euthanasia scares me.' http://www.smh.com.au/comment/im-terminally-ill-and-the-debate-on-euthanasia-scares-me-20170117-gtt0kn.html

Mudie, Ian. 'My Father began as a God' https://fundos.wikispaces.com/file/view/My+Father+Began+as+a+God.pdf

Nash, Sally and Paul Nash. *Tools for reflective ministry.* London: SPCK, 2009.

Native American Legends 'Two Wolves' A Cherokee Legend. http://www.firstpeople.us/FP-Html-Legends/TwoWolves-Cherokee.html

Niklas, Gerald R. *The Making of a Pastoral Person.* New York: Alba House, 2001.

Ormerod, Neil. 'Reconciliation and the Paschal Mystery,' in *A Hunger for Reconciliation.* Gerard Moore (ed.). NSW: St Pauls, 2004:41-53.

Pangrazzi, Arnaldo. *The Art of Caring for the Sick. Guidelines for Creative Ministry,* NY: St Pauls, 2013.

Parnis, Stephen. 'Palliative care the answer.' *In The Australian* July 26th 2017 http://www.theaustralian.com.au/opinion/palliative-care-system-being-starved-of-oxygen/news-story/ca1b4c9b006a3e22e994161d98662ee5

Pastoral Care in Education. Prepared for: Department of Education and Training Western Australia Prepared by: Child Health Promotion Research Unit Edith Cowan University March 2006 http://www.det.wa.edu.au/studentsupport/behaviourandwellbeing/detcms/cms-service/download/asset/?asset_id=8272773

Pattison, Stephen. *The Challenge of Practical Theology. Selected Essays*. London: Jessica Kingsley Publishers, 2007.

Pauw, Amy Plantinga. "Dying well' *in Living Well and Dying Faithfully*, John Swinton and Richard Payne (eds), Grand Rapids, Michigan: William B. Eerdmans Publishing Company, 2009:17-29.

Peterson, Eugene H. *The Contemplative Pastor. Returning to the Art of Spiritual Direction*. Grand Rapids, Michigan: William B. Eerdmans Publishing Company, 1989.

Pope Francis. *Angelus*. St Peter's Square, Sunday, 3 August 2014 https://w2.vatican.va/content/francesco/en/angelus/2014/documents/papa-francesco_angelus_20140803.html

Pope Francis for The 48th World Communications Day

Communication at the Service of an Authentic Culture of Encounter [Sunday, 1 June 2014] https://w2.vatican.va/content/francesco/en/messages/communications/documents/papa-francesco_20140124_messaggio-comunicazioni-sociali.htmlP

Pope Francis, 'Society marginalises the elderly' Address on 15 October 2016, *Catholic News Service* http://www.catholicherald.co.uk/news/2016/10/17/society-is-marginalises-the-elderly-pope-tells-audience-of-grandparents/

Pope John Paul II Letter to the elderly, in 1999, paragraph 10.

https://w2.vatican.va/content/john-paul-ii/en/letters/1999/documents/hf_jp-ii_let_01101999_elderly.html

Powell, John, with Michael H. Cheney. *A Life-Giving Vision: How to be a Christian in Today's World*. Texas: Thomas More, 1995.

Principles for Palliative and End-of-Life Care in Residential Aged Care
http://melbournecatholic.org.au/Portals/0/PCA018_Guiding%20 Principles%20for%20PC%20Aged%20Care_W03.pdf

Purves, Andrew. *Reconstructing Pastoral Theology. A Christological Foundation*, Louisville: Westminster John Knox Press, 2004.

Rahner, Karl. 'God of my Sisters and Brothers,' in *Karl Rahner. Spiritual Writings*. Edited by Philip Endean. Maryknoll: Orbis Books, 2004: 107-111.

Rahner, Karl. *Theological Investigations*, Vol. VII. London: Herder and Herder, 1971.

Reid, Barbara E, 'In her shoes.' *U.S. Catholic*, January 2017: pages 20-24.

Robinson, Geoffrey. *Travels in Sacred Places*. Victoria: Harper Collins Religious, 1997.

Rolheiser, Ronald. *The Holy Longing. The Search for a Christian Spirituality*. New York: Doubleday, 1999.

Rohr, Richard. *What the mystics know. Seven pathways to your deeper self*. New York: The Crossroad Publishing company, 2015.

Rupp, Joyce. *Open the door. A journey to the truth self*. Notre Dame, Indiana: Sorin Books, 2008.

Ryall, Dee. 'We have the power to make death dignified with palliative care.' *Herald Sun*. July 30, 2017.
http://www.heraldsun.com.au/news/opinion/we-have-the-power-to-make-death-dignified-with-palliative-care/news-story/13ea296d3c894 057d05bf3489a749a37

Saad, Marcelo and Roberta de Medeiros. Chapter 7 'Spiritual-Religious Coping – Health Services Empowering Patients' Resources' in *Complementary Therapies for the Contemporary Healthcare. Intech. Open science*. Open minds. Pages 127-144.

Sampson, Alison. *The inevitability of tears*, Eureka Street 2/11/2010 http://www.eurekastreet.com.au/article.aspx?aeid=23722

Shakespeare, William. *Macbeth* Act 4, Scene 3.

Silf, Margaret. *The other side of chaos. Breaking through when life is breaking down*, Chicago: Loyola Press, 2011.

Silvestre, Tesa. *My Mother's Last Spring* A Network for Grateful Living on 12 July 2017 http://www.opw.catholic.org.au/latest-news/my-mother-s-last-spring.html?mc_cid=be645a6a95&mc_eid=33f1f9b328#.WXmEIYiGOU1

Spadaro, Antonio. 'A Big Heart Open to God. The exclusive interview with Pope Francis.' In *Thinking Faith. The online Journal of British Jesuits*.
www.thinkingfaith.org 19th September 2013.

Spivey, John and Shelly Hartwick. 'Grief and Bereavement' in *Hospice, a labor of love*. St. Louis, Missouri: Chalice Press: 1999, 73-85.

Stoddard, Sandol. *The Hospice Movement*. New York: Vintage Books, 1992.

Swift, Christopher. *Hospital Chaplaincy in the Twenty-first Century*, England: Ashgate, 2009.

Truth, Justice and Healing Council. Royal Commission into Institutional Responses to Child Sexual Abuse Issues. Paper No. 2 Towards Healing, 30 September 2013, Paragraph 1.1 http://www.tjhcouncil.org.au/media/39435/30549468_2_TJHC-Towards-Healing-submission-30-Sep-2013.pdf

Valencia, Nick and Devon Sayers, 'Florida teens who recorded drowning man will not be charged in his death' - *CNN.com* July 21st, 2017
http://edition.cnn.com/2017/07/20/us/florida-teens-drowning-man/index.html

Walker, Melissa. Art can heal PTSD's invisible wounds. TED Talks http://www.ted.com/talks/melissa_walker_art_can_heal_ptsd_s_ invisible_wounds/transcript?language=en

What do you say to a homeless person? Advice from Catholic urban missionaries. Catholic News Agency (CNA) Denver, Colo., Sep 23, 2016
http://www.catholicnewsagency.com/news/what-do-you-say-to-a-homeless-person-advice-from-catholic-urban-mission aries-13851/

Wicks, Robert J. *The Inner Life of the Counselor.* New Jersey: John Wiley & Sons, 2012.

Willard W. C. and Ashley, Sr. 'Counseling and Interventions.' In *Professional Spiritual & Pastoral Care: A Practical Clergy and Chaplain's Handbook.* Edited by Stephen B. Roberts. SkyLight Paths Publishing, US, 2013.

Winkler, Jude. *I cry to you, O Lord! Scriptural reflections on the mystery and meaning of suffering.* Maryland: The Word among us Press, 2008.

Yancey, Philip. *What's so amazing about grace?* Grand Rapids: Zondervan, 2000.

www.ingramcontent.com/pod-product-compliance
Lightning Source LLC
Chambersburg PA
CBHW051945290426
44110CB00015B/2119